Your Personal
Horoscope
2017

Libra

G000320533

YOUR PERSONAL HOROSCOPE 2017

LIBRA

24th September–23rd October

igloobooks

igloobooks

Published in 2016
by Igloo Books Ltd
Cottage Farm
Sywell
NN6 0BJ
www.igloobooks.com

Copyright © 2016 Foulsham Publishing Ltd

Produced for Igloo Books by Foulsham Publishing Ltd, The Old Barrel Store,
Drayman's Lane, Marlow, Bucks SL7 2FF, England

FIR003 0716
2 4 6 8 10 9 7 5 3 1
ISBN: 978-1-78557-509-9

This is an abridged version of material originally published
in Old Moore's Horoscope and Astral Diary.

Cover images: iStock
Cover designed by Nicholas Gage

Printed and manufactured in China

CONTENTS

INTRODUCTION

Your Personal Horoscopes have been specifically created to allow you to get the most from astrological patterns and the way they have a bearing on not only your zodiac sign, but nuances within it. Using the diary section of the book you can read about the influences and possibilities of each and every day of the year. It will be possible for you to see when you are likely to be cheerful and happy or those times when your nature is in retreat and you will be more circumspect. The diary will help to give you a feel for the specific 'cycles' of astrology and the way they can subtly change your day-to-day life. For example, when you see the sign ☿, this means that the planet Mercury is retrograde at that time. Retrograde means it appears to be running backwards through the zodiac. Such a happening has a significant effect on communication skills, but this is only one small aspect of how the Personal Horoscope can help you.

With Your Personal Horoscope the story doesn't end with the diary pages. It includes simple ways for you to work out the zodiac sign the Moon occupied at the time of your birth, and what this means for your personality. In addition, if you know the time of day you were born, it is possible to discover your Ascendant, yet another important guide to your personal make-up and potential.

Many readers are interested in relationships and in knowing how well they get on with people of other astrological signs. You might also be interested in the way you appear to very different sorts of individuals. If you are such a person, the section on Venus will be of particular interest. Despite the rapidly changing position of this planet, you can work out your Venus sign, and learn what bearing it will have on your life.

Using Your Personal Horoscope you can travel on one of the most fascinating and rewarding journeys that anyone can take – the journey to a better realisation of self.

THE ESSENCE
OF LIBRA

Exploring the Personality of Libra the Scales
(24TH SEPTEMBER–23RD OCTOBER)

What's in a sign?

At heart you may be the least complicated of all the zodiac sign types, though your ruling element is Air, and that is always going to supply some surprises. Diplomatic, kind and affectionate, your nature blows like a refreshing breeze through the lives of almost anyone you meet. It isn't like you to be gloomy for very long at a time, and you know how to influence the world around you.

It's true that you don't like dirt, or too much disorganisation, and you tend to be very artistic by inclination. You get your own way in life, not by dint of making yourself unpopular in any way but rather with the sort of gentle persuasion to which almost everyone you know falls victim at one time or another. Being considerate of others is more or less second nature to you, though you may not be quite as self-sacrificing as sometimes appears to be the case. You definitely know what you want from life and are not above using a little subterfuge when it comes to getting it.

You are capable and resourceful, but just a little timid on occasions. All the same, when dealing with subject matter that you know and relish, few can better you out there in the practical world. You know how to order your life and can be just as successful in a career sense as you tend to be in your home life. There are times when personal attractions can be something of a stumbling block because you love readily and are very influenced by the kindness and compliments of those around you.

Librans do need to plan ahead, but don't worry about this fact too much because you are also extremely good at thinking on your feet. Getting others to do your bidding is a piece of cake because you are not tardy when it comes to showing your affections. Nevertheless you need to be careful not to allow yourself to fall into unreliable company, or to get involved in schemes that seem too good to be true – some of them are. But for most of the time you present a happy picture to the world and get along just fine, with your ready smile and adaptable personality. You leave almost any situation happier and more contented than it was when you arrived.

Libra resources

When it comes to getting on in life you have as much ammunition in your armoury as most zodiac signs and a great deal more than some. For starters you are adaptable and very resourceful. When you have to take a leap in logic there is nothing preventing you from doing so, and the strong intuition of which your zodiac sign is capable can prove to be very useful at times.

One of your strongest points is the way you manage to make others love you. Although you might consider yourself to be distinctly 'ordinary', that's not the way the world at large perceives you. Most Librans have the ability to etch themselves onto the minds of practically everyone they come across. Why? It's simple. You listen to what people have to say and appear to be deeply interested. On most occasions you are, but even if the tale is a tedious one you give the impression of being rooted to the spot with a determination to hear the story right through. When it comes to responding you are extremely diplomatic and always manage to steer a sensible course between any two or more opposing factions.

Having said that you don't like dirt or untidy places, this is another fact that you can turn to your advantage, because you can always find someone who will help you out. So charming can Libra be that those who do all they can to make you more comfortable regularly end up feeling that you have done them a favour.

It is the sheer magic of the understated Libran that does the trick every time. Even on those rare occasions when you go out with all guns blazing to get what you want from life, you are very unlikely to make enemies on the way. Of course you do have to be careful on occasions, like everyone, but you can certainly push issues further than most. Why? Mainly because people don't realise that you are doing so.

You could easily sell any commodity – though it might be necessary to believe in it yourself first. Since you can always see the good points in anything and tend to be generally optimistic, that should not be too problematical either.

Beneath the surface

In many respects Libra could be the least complicated sign of the zodiac so it might be assumed that 'what you see is what you get'. Life is rarely quite that simple, though you are one of the most straightforward people when it comes to inner struggle. The fact is that most Librans simply don't have a great deal. Between subconscious motivation and in-your-face action there is a seamless process. Librans do need to be loved and this fact can be quite a strong motivation in itself towards any particular course of action. However, even this desire for affection isn't the most powerful factor when considering the sign of the Scales.

What matters most to you is balance, which is probably not at all surprising considering what your zodiac sign actually means. Because of this you would go to tremendous lengths to make sure that your inner resolves create the right external signs and actions to offer the peace that you are looking for most of all.

Like most people born under the Air signs you are not quite as confident as you sometimes appear to be. In the main you are modest and not given to boasting, so you don't attract quite the level of attention of your fellow Air signs, Gemini and Aquarius. All the same you are quite capable of putting on an act when it's necessary to give a good account of yourself in public. You could be quaking inside but you do have the ability to hide this from the world at large.

Librans exhibit such a strong desire to be kind to everyone they meet that they may hide their inner feelings from some people altogether. It's important to remember to be basically honest, even if that means upsetting others a little. This is the most difficult trait for Libra to deal with and may go part of the way to explaining why so many relationship break-ups occur for people born under this zodiac sign. However, as long as you find ways and means to explain your deepest emotional needs, at least to those you love, all should be well.

In most respects you tend to be an open book, particularly to those who take the trouble to look. Your nature is not over-deep, and you are almost certainly not on some secret search to find the 'real you'. Although Libra is sometimes accused of being superficial there are many people in the world who would prefer simplicity to complications and duplicity.

Making the best of yourself

This may be the easiest category by far for the zodiac sign of Libra. The fact is that you rarely do anything else but offer the best version of what you are. Presentation is second nature to Libra, which just loves to be noticed. Despite this you are naturally modest and so not inclined to go over the top in company. You can be relied upon to say and do the right things for most of the time. Even when you consider your actions to be zany and perhaps less acceptable, this is not going to be the impression that the majority of people would get.

In a work sense you need to be involved in some sort of occupation that is clean, allows for a sense of order and ultimately offers the ability to use your head as well as your hands. The fact is that you don't care too much for unsavoury sorts of work and need to be in an environment that suits your basically refined nature. If the circumstances are right you can give a great deal to your work and will go far. Librans also need to be involved with others because they are natural co-operators. For this reason you may not be at your best when working alone or in situations that necessitate all the responsibilities being exclusively yours.

When in the social mainstream you tend to make the best of yourself by simply being what you naturally are. You don't need frills and fancies. Libra is able to make the best sort of impression by using the natural qualities inherent in the sign. As a result, your natural poise, your ability to cut through social divisions, your intelligence and your adaptability should all ensure that you remain popular.

What may occasionally prove difficult is being quite as dominant as the world assumes you ought to be. Many people equate efficiency with power. This is not the way of people born under the Scales, and you need to make that fact plain to anyone who seems to have the desire to shape you.

The impressions you give

Although the adage 'what you see is what you get' may be truer for Libra than for any of its companion signs, it can't be exclusively the case. However, under almost all circumstances you are likely to make friends. You are a much shrewder operator than sometimes appears to be the case and tend to weigh things in the balance very carefully. Libra can be most things to most people, and that's the sort of adaptability that ensures success at both a social and a professional level.

The chances are that you are already well respected and deeply liked by most of the people you know. This isn't so surprising since you are not inclined to make waves of any sort. Whether or not this leads to you achieving the degree of overall success that you deserve in life is quite a different matter. When impressions count you don't tend to let yourself down, or the people who rely on you. Adapting yourself to suit different circumstances is the meat and drink of your basic nature and you have plenty of poise and charm to disarm even the most awkward of people.

In affairs of the heart you are equally adept at putting others at their ease. There is very little difficulty involved in getting people to show their affection for you and when it comes to romance you are one of the most successful practitioners to be found anywhere. The only slight problem in this area of life, as with others, is that you are so talented at offering people what they want that you might not always be living the sort of life that genuinely suits you. Maybe giving the right impression is a little too important for Libra. A deeper form of honesty from the start would prevent you from having to show a less charming side to your nature in the end.

In most circumstances you can be relied upon to exhibit a warm, affectionate, kind, sincere and interesting face to the world at large. As long as this underpins truthfulness it's hard to understand how Libra could really go far wrong.

The way forward

You must already be fairly confident that you have the necessary skills and natural abilities to get on well in a world that is also filled with other people. From infancy most Librans learn how to rub along with others, whilst offering every indication that they are both adaptable and amenable to change. Your chameleon-like ability to 'change colour' in order to suit prevailing circumstances means that you occasionally drop back to being part of the wallpaper in the estimation of at least some people. A greater ability to make an impression probably would not go amiss sometimes, but making a big fuss isn't your way and you actively seek an uncomplicated sort of life.

Balance is everything to Libra, a fact that means there are times when you end up with nothing at all. What needs to be remembered is that there are occasions when everyone simply has to make a decision. This is the hardest thing in the world for you to do but when you manage it you become even more noticed by the world at large.

There's no doubt that people generally hold you in great affection. They know you to be quite capable and love your easy-going attitude to life. You are rarely judgmental and tend to offer almost anyone the benefit of the doubt. Although you are chatty, and inclined to listen avidly to gossip, it isn't your natural way to be unkind, caustic or backbiting. As a result it would seem that you have all the prerequisites to live an extremely happy life. Alas, things are rarely quite that easy.

It is very important for you to demonstrate to yourself, as well as to others, that you are an individual with thoughts and feelings of your own. So often do you defer to the needs of those around you that the real you gets somewhat squashed on the way. There have to be times when you are willing to say 'yes' or 'no' unequivocally, instead of a noncommittal 'I don't really mind' or 'whatever you think best'. At the end of the day you do have opinions and can lead yourself into the path of some severe frustrations if you are unwilling to voice them in the first place.

Try to be particularly honest in deep, emotional attachments. Many Libran relationships come to grief simply because there isn't enough earthy honesty present in the first place. People knowing how you feel won't make them care for you any less. A fully integrated, truthful Libran, with a willingness to participate in the decision making, turns out to be the person who is both successful and happy.

LIBRA ON THE CUSP

Astrological profiles are altered for those people born at either the beginning or the end of a zodiac sign, or, more properly, on the cusps of a sign. In the case of Libra this would be on the 24th of September and for two or three days after, and similarly at the end of the sign, probably from the 21st to the 23rd of October.

The Virgo Cusp – 24th to 26th September

Here we find a Libran subject with a greater than average sense of responsibility and probably a better potential for success than is usually the case for Libra when taken alone. The Virgoan tendency to take itself rather too seriously is far less likely when the sign is mixed with Libra and the resultant nature is often deeply inspiring, and yet quite centred. The Virgo-cusp Libran has what it takes to break through the red tape of society, and yet can understand the need for its existence in the first place. You are caring and concerned, quick on the uptake and very ready to listen to any point of view but, at the end of the day, you know when it is going to be necessary to take a personal stance and this you are far more willing to do than would be the case for non-cuspid Librans.

Family members are important to you, but you always allow them their own individuality and won't get in the way of their personal need to spread their own wings, even at times when it's hard to take this positive stance. Practically speaking, you are a good home-maker but you also enjoy travelling and can benefit greatly from seeing the way other cultures think and behave. It is true that you can have the single-mindedness of a Virgoan, but even this aspect is modified by the Libran within you, so that you usually try to see alternative points of view and often succeed in doing so.

At work you really come into your own. Not only are you capable enough to deal with just about any eventuality, you are also willing to be flexible and to make up your mind instantly when it proves necessary to do so. Colleagues and subordinates alike tend to trust you. You may consider self-employment, unlike most Librans who are usually very worried by this prospect. Making your way in life is something you tend to take for granted, even when the going gets tough.

What people most like about you is that, despite your tremendously practical approach to life, you can be very zany and retain a sense of fun that is, at its best, second to none. Few people find you difficult to understand or to get on with in a day-to-day sense.

The Scorpio Cusp – 21st to 23rd October

The main difference between this cusp and the one at the Virgo end of Libra, is that you tend to be more emotionally motivated and of a slightly less practical nature. Routines are easy for you to address, though you can become very restless and tend to find your own emotional responses difficult to deal with. Sometimes even you don't understand what makes you tick, and that can be a problem. Actually you are not as complicated as you may have come to believe. It's simply that you have a unique view of life and one that doesn't always match that of the people around you, but as Libra instinctively wants to conform, this can lead to some personal confusion.

In family matters you are responsible, very caring and deeply committed to others. It's probable that you work in some field that finds you in direct contact with the public at large and many Scorpio-cusp Librans choose welfare, social or hospital work as a first choice. When it comes to love, you are flexible in your choice and the necessary attributes to promote a long-lasting and happy relationship are clearly present in your basic nature. If there are problems, they may come about as a result of your inability to choose properly in the first place, because you are the first to offer anyone the benefit of the doubt.

When it comes to the practicalities of life, Scorpio can prove to be extremely useful. It offers an 'edge' to your nature and, as Scorpio is a Fixed sign, you are less likely to lose ground because of lack of confidence than Libra alone would be. Your future can be bright, but only if you are willing to get involved in something that really interests you in the first place. You certainly do not care for getting your hands dirty and tend to gravitate towards more refined positions.

Creative potential is good and you could be very artistic, though if this extends to fine art, at least some of your pictures will have 'dark' overtones that might shock some people, including yourself. At base you are kind, caring, complicated, yet inspiring.

LIBRA AND ITS ASCENDANTS

The nature of every individual on the planet is composed of the rich variety of zodiac signs and planetary positions that were present at the time of their birth. Your Sun sign, which in your case is Libra, is one of the many factors when it comes to assessing the unique person you are. Probably the most important consideration, other than your Sun sign, is to establish the zodiac sign that was rising over the eastern horizon at the time that you were born. This is your Ascending or Rising sign. Most popular astrology fails to take account of the Ascendant, and yet its importance remains with you from the very moment of your birth, through every day of your life. The Ascendant is evident in the way you approach the world, and so, when meeting a person for the first time, it is this astrological influence that you are most likely to notice first. Our Ascending sign essentially represents what we appear to be, while the Sun sign is what we feel inside ourselves.

The Ascendant also has the potential for modifying our overall nature. For example, if you were born at a time of day when Libra was passing over the eastern horizon (this would be around the time of dawn) then you would be classed as a double Libran. As such, you would typify this zodiac sign, both internally and in your dealings with others. However, if your Ascendant sign turned out to be a Water sign, such as Pisces, there would be a profound alteration of nature, away from the expected qualities of Libra.

One of the reasons why popular astrology often ignores the Ascendant is that it has always been rather difficult to establish. We have found a way to make this possible by devising an easy-to-use table, which you will find on page 157 of this book. Using this, you can establish your Ascendant sign at a glance. You will need to know your rough time of birth, then it is simply a case of following the instructions.

For those readers who have no idea of their time of birth it might be worth allowing a good friend, or perhaps your partner, to read through the section that follows this introduction. Someone who deals with you on a regular basis may easily discover your Ascending sign, even though you could have some difficulty establishing it for yourself. A good understanding of this component of your nature is essential if you want to be aware of that 'other person' who is responsible for the way you make contact with the world at large. Your Sun sign, Ascendant sign, and the other pointers in this book

17

will, together, allow you a far better understanding of what makes you tick as an individual. Peeling back the different layers of your astrological make-up can be an enlightening experience, and the Ascendant may represent one of the most important layers of all.

Libra with Libra Ascendant

There is no doubt that you carry the very best of all Libran worlds in your nature, though at the same time there is a definite possibility that you often fall between two stools. The literal advice as a result is that you must sometimes make a decision, even though it isn't all that easy for you to do so. Not everyone understands your easy-going side and there are occasions when you could appear to be too flippant for your own good.

The way you approach the world makes you popular, and there is no doubt at all that you are the most diplomatic person to be found anywhere in the length and breadth of the zodiac. It is your job in life to stop people disagreeing and since you can always see every point of view, you make a good impression on the way.

Relationships can sometimes be awkward for you because you can change your mind so easily. But love is never lacking and you can be fairly certain of a generally happy life. Over-indulging is always a potential problem for Air-sign people such as yourself, and there are times in your life when you must get the rest and relaxation which is so important in funding a strong nervous system. Drink plenty of water to flush out a system that can be over-high in natural salts.

Libra with Scorpio Ascendant

There is some tendency for you to be far more deep than the average Libran would appear to be, and for this reason it is crucial that you lighten up from time to time. Every person with a Scorpio quality needs to remember that there is a happy and carefree side to all events, and your Libran quality should allow you to bear this in mind. Sometimes you try to do too many things at the same time. This is fine if you take the casual overview of Libra, but less sensible when you insist on picking the last bone out of every potential, as is much more the case for Scorpio.

When worries come along, as they sometimes will, be able to listen to what your friends have to say and also realise that they are more than willing to work on your behalf, if only because you are so loyal to them. You do have a quality of self-deception, but this should not get in the way too much if you combine the instinctive actions of Libra with the deep intuition of your Scorpio component.

Probably the most important factor of this combination is your ability to succeed in a financial sense. You make a good manager, but not of the authoritarian sort. Jobs in the media or where you are expected to make up your mind quickly would suit you because there is always an underpinning of practical sense that rarely lets you down.

Libra with Sagittarius Ascendant

A very happy combination this, with a great desire for life in all its forms and a need to push forward the bounds of the possible in a way that few other zodiac sign connections would do. You don't like the unpleasant or ugly in life and yet you are capable of dealing with both if you have to. Giving so much to humanity, you still manage to retain a degree of individuality that would surprise many, charm others, and please all.

On the reverse side of the same coin you might find that you are sometimes accused of being fickle, but this is only an expression of your need for change and variety, which is endemic to both these signs. True, you have more of a temper than would be the case for Libra when taken on its own, but such incidents would see you up and down in a flash, and it is almost impossible for you to bear a grudge of any sort. Routines get on your nerves and you are far happier when you can please yourself and get ahead at your own pace, which is quite fast.

As a lover you can make a big impression and most of you will not go short of affection in the early days, before you choose to commit yourself. Once you do, there is always a chance of romantic problems, but these are less likely when you have chosen carefully in the first place.

Libra with Capricorn Ascendant

It is a fact that Libra is the most patient of the Air signs, though like the others it needs to get things done fairly quickly. Capricorn, on the other hand, will work long and hard to achieve its objectives and will not be thwarted in the end. As a result this is a quite powerful sign combination and one that should lead to ultimate success.

Capricorn is often accused of taking itself too seriously and yet it has an ironic and really very funny sense of humour which only its chief confidants recognise. Libra is lighthearted, always willing to have fun and quite anxious to please. When these two basic types come together in their best forms, you might find yourself to be one of the most well-balanced people around. Certainly you know what you want, but you don't have to use a bulldozer in order to get it.

Active and enthusiastic when something really takes your fancy, you might also turn out to be one of the very best lovers of them all. The reason for this is that you have the depth of Capricorn but the lighter and more directly affectionate qualities of the Scales. What you want from life in a personal sense, you eventually tend to get, but you don't care too much if this takes you a while. Few people could deny that you are a faithful friend, a happy sort and a deeply magnetic personality.

Libra with Aquarius Ascendant

Stand by for a truly interesting and very inspiring combination here, but one that is sometimes rather difficult to fathom, even for the sort of people who believe themselves to be very perceptive. The reason for this could be that any situation has to be essentially fixed and constant in order to get a handle on it, and this is certainly not the case for the Aquarian–Libran type. The fact is that both these signs are Air signs, and to a certain extent as unpredictable as the wind itself.

To most people you seem to be original, frank, free and very outspoken. Not everything you do makes sense to others, and if you were alive during the hippy era, it is likely that you went around with flowers in your hair, for you are a free-thinking idealist at heart. With age you mature somewhat, but never too much, because you will always see the strange, the comical and the original in life. This is what keeps you young and is one of the factors that makes you so very attractive to members of the opposite sex. Many people will want to 'adopt' you, and you are at your very best when in company.

Much of your effort is expounded on others and yet, unless you discipline yourself a good deal, personal relationships of the romantic sort can bring certain difficulties. Careful planning is necessary.

Libra with Pisces Ascendant

An Air and Water combination, you are not easy to understand and have depths that show at times, surprising those people who thought they already knew what you were. You will always keep people guessing and are just as likely to hitchhike around Europe as you are to hold down a steady job, both of which you would undertake with the same degree of commitment and success. Usually young at heart, but always carrying the potential for an old head on young shoulders, you are something of a paradox and not at all easy for totally 'straight' types to understand. But you always make an impression and tend to be very attractive to members of the opposite sex.

In matters of health you do have to be a little careful because you dissipate much nervous energy and can sometimes be inclined to push yourself too hard, at least in a mental sense. Frequent periods of rest and meditation will do you the world of good and should improve your level of wisdom, which tends to be fairly high already. Much of your effort in life is expounded on behalf of humanity as a whole, for you care deeply, love totally and always give of your best. Whatever your faults and failings might be, you are one of the most popular people around.

Libra with Aries Ascendant

Libra has the tendency to bring out the best in any zodiac sign, and this is no exception when it comes together with Aries. You may, in fact, be the most comfortable of all Aries types, simply because Libra tempers some of your more assertive qualities and gives you the chance to balance out opposing forces, both inside yourself and in the world outside. You are fun to be with and make the staunchest friend possible. Although you are generally affable, few people would try to put one over on you because they would quickly come to know how far you are willing to go before you let forth a string of invective that would shock those who previously underestimated your basic Aries traits.

Home and family are very dear to you, but you are more tolerant than some Aries types are inclined to be and you have a youthful zest for life that should stay with you no matter what age you manage to achieve. There is always something interesting to do and your mind is a constant stream of possibilities. This makes you very creative and you may also demonstrate a desire to look good at all times. You may not always be quite as confident as you appear to be, but few would guess the fact.

Libra with Taurus Ascendant

A fortunate combination in many ways, this is a double-Venus rulership, since both Taurus and Libra are heavily reliant on the planet of love. You are social, amiable and a natural diplomat, anxious to please and ready to care for just about anyone who shows interest in you. You hate disorder, which means that there is a place for everything and everything in its place. This can throw up the odd paradox however, since being half Libran you cannot always work out where that place ought to be! You deal with life in a humorous way and are quite capable of seeing the absurd in yourself, as well as in others. Your heart is no bigger than that of the quite typical Taurean, but it sits rather closer to the surface and so others recognise it more.

On those occasions when you know you are standing on firm ground you can show great confidence, even if you have to be ready to change some of your opinions at the drop of a hat. When this happens you can be quite at odds with yourself, because Taurus doesn't take very many U-turns, whereas Libra does. Don't expect to know yourself too well, and keep looking for the funny side of things, because it is within humour that you forge the sort of life that suits you best.

Libra with Gemini Ascendant

What a happy-go-lucky soul you are and how popular you tend to be with those around you. Libra is, like Gemini, an Air sign and this means that you are the communicator par excellence, even by Gemini standards. It can sometimes be difficult for you to make up your mind about things because Libra does not exactly aid this process, and especially not when it is allied to Mercurial Gemini. Frequent periods of deep thought are necessary, and meditation would do you a great deal of good. All the same, although you might sometimes be rather unsure of yourself, you are rarely without a certain balance. Clean and tidy surroundings suit you the best, though this is far from easy to achieve because you are invariably dashing off to some place or other, so you really need someone to sort things out in your absence.

The most important fact of all is that you are much loved by your friends, of which there are likely to be very many. Because you are so willing to help them out, in return they are usually there when it matters and they would probably go to almost any length on your behalf. You exhibit a fine sense of justice and will usually back those in trouble. Charities tend to be attractive to you and you do much on behalf of those who live on the fringes of society or people who are truly alone.

Libra with Cancer Ascendant

What an absolutely pleasant and approachable sort of person you are, and how much you have to offer. Like most people associated with the sign of Cancer you give yourself freely to the world, and will always be on hand if anyone is in trouble or needs the special touch you can bring to almost any problem. Behaving in this way is the biggest part of what you are and so people come to rely on you very heavily. Like Libra you can see both sides of any coin and you exhibit the Libran tendency to jump about from one foot to the other when it is necessary to make decisions relating to your own life. This is not usually the case when you are dealing with others however, because the cooler and more detached qualities of Cancer will show through in these circumstances.

It would be fair to say that you do not deal with routines as well as Cancer alone might do and you need a degree of variety in your life, which in your case often comes in the form of travel, which can be distant and of long duration. It isn't unusual for people who have this zodiac combination to end up living abroad, though even this does little to prevent you from getting itchy feet from time to time. In romance you show an original quality that keeps the relationship young and working very well.

Libra with Leo Ascendant

Libra brings slightly more flexibility to the fixed quality of the Leo nature. On the whole you do not represent a picture that is so much different from other versions of the Lion, though you find more time to smile, enjoy changing your mind a great deal more and have a greater number of casual friends. Few would find you proud or haughty and you retain the common touch that can be so important when it comes to getting on in life generally. At work you like to do something that brings variety, and would probably soon tire of doing the same task over and over again. Many of you are teachers, for you have patience, allied to a stubborn core. This can be an indispensable combination on occasions and is part of the reason for the material success that many folk with this combination of signs achieve.

It isn't often that you get down in the dumps, after all there is generally something more important around the next corner, and you love the cut and thrust of everyday life. You always manage to stay young at heart, no matter what your age might be, and you revel in the company of interesting and stimulating types. Maybe you should try harder to concentrate on one thing at once and also strive to retain a serious opinion for more than ten minutes at a time. However, Leo helps to control your flighty tendencies.

Libra with Virgo Ascendant

Libra has the ability to lighten almost any load, and it is particularly good at doing so when it is brought together with the much more repressed sign of Virgo. To the world at large you seem relaxed, happy and able to cope with most of the pressures that life places upon you. Not only do you deal with your own life in a bright and breezy manner but you are usually on hand to help others out of any dilemma that they might make for themselves. With excellent powers of communication, you leave the world at large in no doubt whatsoever concerning both your opinions and your wishes. It is in the talking stakes that you really excel because Virgo brings the silver tongue of Mercury and Libra adds the Air-sign desire to be in constant touch with the world outside your door.

You like to have a good time and can often be found in the company of interesting and stimulating people, who have the ability to bring out the very best in your bright and sparkling personality. Underneath however, there is still much of the worrying Virgoan to be found and this means that you have to learn to relax inside as well as appearing to do so externally. In fact you are much more complex than most people would realise, and definitely would not be suited to a life that allowed you too much time to think about yourself.

THE MOON AND THE PART IT PLAYS IN YOUR LIFE

In astrology the Moon is probably the single most important heavenly body after the Sun. Its unique position, as partner to the Earth on its journey around the solar system, means that the Moon appears to pass through the signs of the zodiac extremely quickly. The zodiac position of the Moon at the time of your birth plays a great part in personal character and is especially significant in the build-up of your emotional nature.

Your Own Moon Sign

Discovering the position of the Moon at the time of your birth has always been notoriously difficult because tracking the complex zodiac positions of the Moon is not easy. This process has been reduced to three simple stages with our Lunar Tables. A breakdown of the Moon's zodiac positions can be found from page 35 onwards, so that once you know what your Moon Sign is, you can see what part this plays in the overall build-up of your personal character.

If you follow the instructions on the next page you will soon be able to work out exactly what zodiac sign the Moon occupied on the day that you were born and you can then go on to compare the reading for this position with those of your Sun sign and your Ascendant. It is partly the comparison between these three important positions that goes towards making you the unique individual you are.

HOW TO DISCOVER YOUR MOON SIGN

This is a three-stage process. You may need a pen and a piece of paper but if you follow the instructions below the process should only take a minute or so.

STAGE 1 First of all you need to know the Moon Age at the time of your birth. If you look at Moon Table 1, on page 33, you will find all the years between 1919 and 2017 down the left side. Find the year of your birth and then trace across to the right to the month of your birth. Where the two intersect you will find a number. This is the date of the New Moon in the month that you were born. You now need to count forward the number of days between the New Moon and your own birthday. For example, if the New Moon in the month of your birth was shown as being the 6th and you were born on the 20th, your Moon Age Day would be 14. If the New Moon in the month of your birth came after your birthday, you need to count forward from the New Moon in the previous month. Whatever the result, jot this number down so that you do not forget it.

STAGE 2 Take a look at Moon Table 2 on page 34. Down the left hand column look for the date of your birth. Now trace across to the month of your birth. Where the two meet you will find a letter. Copy this letter down alongside your Moon Age Day.

STAGE 3 Moon Table 3 on page 34 will supply you with the zodiac sign the Moon occupied on the day of your birth. Look for your Moon Age Day down the left hand column and then for the letter you found in Stage 2. Where the two converge you will find a zodiac sign and this is the sign occupied by the Moon on the day that you were born.

Your Zodiac Moon Sign Explained

You will find a profile of all zodiac Moon Signs on pages 35 to 38, showing in yet another way how astrology helps to make you into the individual that you are. In each daily entry of the Astral Diary you can find the zodiac position of the Moon for every day of the year. This also allows you to discover your lunar birthdays. Since the Moon passes through all the signs of the zodiac in about a month, you can expect something like twelve lunar birthdays each year. At these times you are likely to be emotionally steady and able to make the sort of decisions that have real, lasting value.

MOON TABLE 1

YEAR	AUG	SEP	OCT	YEAR	AUG	SEP	OCT	YEAR	AUG	SEP	OCT
1919	25	23	23	1952	20	19	18	1985	16	14	14
1920	14	12	12	1953	9	8	8	1986	5	4	3
1921	3	2	1/30	1954	28	27	26	1987	24	23	22
1922	22	21	20	1955	17	16	15	1988	12	11	10
1923	12	10	10	1956	6	4	4	1989	1/31	29	29
1924	30	28	28	1957	25	23	23	1990	20	19	18
1925	19	18	17	1958	15	13	12	1991	9	8	8
1926	8	7	6	1959	4	3	2/31	1992	28	26	25
1927	27	25	25	1960	22	21	20	1993	17	16	15
1928	16	14	14	1961	11	10	9	1994	7	5	5
1929	5	3	2	1962	30	28	28	1995	26	24	24
1930	24	22	20	1963	19	17	17	1996	14	13	11
1931	13	12	11	1964	7	6	5	1997	3	2	2/31
1932	2/31	30	29	1965	26	25	24	1998	22	20	20
1933	21	19	19	1966	16	14	14	1999	11	10	8
1934	10	9	8	1967	5	4	3	2000	29	27	27
1935	29	27	27	1968	24	23	22	2001	19	17	17
1936	17	15	15	1969	12	11	10	2002	8	6	6
1937	6	4	4	1970	2	1	1/30	2003	27	26	25
1938	25	23	23	1971	20	19	19	2004	14	13	12
1939	15	13	12	1972	9	8	8	2005	4	3	2
1940	4	2	1/30	1973	28	27	26	2006	23	22	21
1941	22	21	20	1974	17	16	15	2007	13	12	11
1942	12	10	10	1975	7	5	5	2008	1/31	30	29
1943	1/30	29	29	1976	25	23	23	2009	20	19	18
1944	18	17	17	1977	14	13	12	2010	10	8	8
1945	8	6	6	1978	4	2	2/31	2011	29	27	27
1946	26	25	24	1979	22	21	20	2012	17	16	15
1947	16	14	14	1980	11	10	9	2013	6	4	4
1948	5	3	2	1981	29	28	27	2014	24	23	22
1949	24	23	21	1982	19	17	17	2015	15	13	12
1950	13	12	11	1983	8	7	6	2016	2	1	30
1951	2	1	1/30	1984	26	25	24	2017	22	20	20

33

TABLE 2

DAY	SEP	OCT
1	X	a
2	X	a
3	X	a
4	Y	b
5	Y	b
6	Y	b
7	Y	b
8	Y	b
9	Y	b
10	Y	b
11	Y	b
12	Y	b
13	Y	b
14	Z	d
15	Z	d
16	Z	d
17	Z	d
18	Z	d
19	Z	d
20	Z	d
21	Z	d
22	Z	d
23	Z	d
24	a	e
25	a	e
26	a	e
27	a	e
28	a	e
29	a	e
30	a	e
31	–	e

MOON TABLE 3

M/D	X	Y	Z	a	b	d	e
0	VI	VI	LI	LI	LI	LI	SC
1	VI	LI	LI	LI	LI	SC	SC
2	LI	LI	LI	LI	SC	SC	SC
3	LI	LI	SC	SC	SC	SC	SA
4	LI	SC	SC	SC	SA	SA	SA
5	SC	SC	SC	SA	SA	SA	CP
6	SC	SA	SA	SA	CP	CP	CP
7	SA	SA	SA	SA	CP	CP	AQ
8	SA	SA	CP	CP	CP	CP	AQ
9	SA	CP	CP	CP	AQ	AQ	AQ
10	CP	CP	CP	AQ	AQ	AQ	PI
11	CP	AQ	AQ	AQ	PI	PI	PI
12	AQ	AQ	AQ	PI	PI	PI	AR
13	AQ	AQ	PI	PI	AR	PI	AR
14	PI	PI	PI	AR	AR	AR	TA
15	PI	PI	PI	AR	AR	AR	TA
16	PI	AR	AR	AR	AR	TA	TA
17	AR	AR	AR	AR	TA	TA	GE
18	AR	AR	AR	TA	TA	GE	GE
19	AR	TA	TA	TA	TA	GE	GE
20	TA	TA	TA	GE	GE	GE	CA
21	TA	GE	GE	GE	GE	CA	CA
22	GE	GE	GE	GE	CA	CA	CA
23	GE	GE	GE	CA	CA	CA	LE
24	GE	CA	CA	CA	CA	LE	LE
25	CA	CA	CA	CA	LE	LE	LE
26	CA	LE	LE	LE	LE	VI	VI
27	LE	LE	LE	LE	VI	VI	VI
28	LE	LE	LE	VI	VI	VI	LI
29	LE	VI	VI	VI	VI	LI	LI

AR = Aries, TA = Taurus, GE = Gemini, CA = Cancer, LE = Leo, VI = Virgo,
LI = Libra, SC = Scorpio, SA = Sagittarius, CP = Capricorn, AQ = Aquarius, PI = Pisces

MOON SIGNS

Moon in Aries

You have a strong imagination, courage, determination and a desire to do things in your own way and forge your own path through life.

Originality is a key attribute; you are seldom stuck for ideas although your mind is changeable and you could take the time to focus on individual tasks. Often quick-tempered, you take orders from few people and live life at a fast pace. Avoid health problems by taking regular time out for rest and relaxation.

Emotionally, it is important that you talk to those you are closest to and work out your true feelings. Once you discover that people are there to help, there is less necessity for you to do everything yourself.

Moon in Taurus

The Moon in Taurus gives you a courteous and friendly manner, which means you are likely to have many friends.

The good things in life mean a lot to you, as Taurus is an Earth sign that delights in experiences which please the senses. Hence you are probably a lover of good food and drink, which may in turn mean you need to keep an eye on the bathroom scales, especially as looking good is also important to you.

Emotionally you are fairly stable and you stick by your own standards. Taureans do not respond well to change. Intuition also plays an important part in your life.

Moon in Gemini

You have a warm-hearted character, sympathetic and eager to help others. At times reserved, you can also be articulate and chatty: this is part of the paradox of Gemini, which always brings duplicity to the nature. You are interested in current affairs, have a good intellect, and are good company and likely to have many friends. Most of your friends have a high opinion of you and would be ready to defend you should the need arise. However, this is usually unnecessary, as you are quite capable of defending yourself in any verbal confrontation.

Travel is important to your inquisitive mind and you find intellectual stimulus in mixing with people from different cultures. You also gain much from reading, writing and the arts but you do need plenty of rest and relaxation in order to avoid fatigue.

Moon in Cancer

The Moon in Cancer at the time of birth is a fortunate position as Cancer is the Moon's natural home. This means that the qualities of compassion and understanding given by the Moon are especially enhanced in your nature, and you are friendly and sociable and cope well with emotional pressures. You cherish home and family life, and happily do the domestic tasks. Your surroundings are important to you and you hate squalor and filth. You are likely to have a love of music and poetry.

Your basic character, although at times changeable like the Moon itself, depends on symmetry. You aim to make your surroundings comfortable and harmonious, for yourself and those close to you.

Moon in Leo

The best qualities of the Moon and Leo come together to make you warm-hearted, fair, ambitious and self-confident. With good organisational abilities, you invariably rise to a position of responsibility in your chosen career. This is fortunate as you don't enjoy being an 'also-ran' and would rather be an important part of a small organisation than a menial in a large one.

You should be lucky in love, and happy, provided you put in the effort to make a comfortable home for yourself and those close to you. It is likely that you will have a love of pleasure, sport, music and literature. Life brings you many rewards, most of them as a direct result of your own efforts, although you may be luckier than average and ready to make the best of any situation.

Moon in Virgo

You are endowed with good mental abilities and a keen receptive memory, but you are never ostentatious or pretentious. Naturally quite reserved, you still have many friends, especially of the opposite sex. Marital relationships must be discussed carefully and worked at so that they remain harmonious, as personal attachments can be a problem if you do not give them your full attention.

Talented and persevering, you possess artistic qualities and are a good homemaker. Earning your honours through genuine merit, you work long and hard towards your objectives but show little pride in your achievements. Many short journeys will be undertaken in your life.

Moon in Libra

With the Moon in Libra you are naturally popular and make friends
easily. People like you, probably more than you realise, you bring fun
to a party and are a natural diplomat. For all its good points, Libra is
not the most stable of astrological signs and, as a result, your emotions
can be a little unstable too. Therefore, although the Moon in Libra is
said to be good for love and marriage, your Sun sign and Rising sign
will have an important effect on your emotional and loving qualities.

You must remember to relate to others in your decision-making.
Co-operation is crucial because Libra represents the 'balance' of
life that can only be achieved through harmonious relationships.
Conformity is not easy for you because Libra, an Air sign, likes its
independence.

Moon in Scorpio

Some people might call you pushy. In fact, all you really want to do
is to live life to the full and protect yourself and your family from the
pressures of life. Take care to avoid giving the impression of being
sarcastic or impulsive and use your energies wisely and constructively.

You have great courage and you invariably achieve your goals by
force of personality and sheer effort. You are fond of mystery and
are good at predicting the outcome of situations and events. Travel
experiences can be beneficial to you.

You may experience problems if you do not take time to examine
your motives in a relationship, and also if you allow jealousy, always
a feature of Scorpio, to cloud your judgement.

Moon in Sagittarius

The Moon in Sagittarius helps to make you a generous individual with
humanitarian qualities and a kind heart. Restlessness may be intrinsic
as your mind is seldom still. Perhaps because of this, you have a need
for change that could lead you to several major moves during your
adult life. You are not afraid to stand your ground when you know
your judgement is right, you speak directly and have good intuition.

At work you are quick, efficient and versatile and so you make an
ideal employee. You need work to be intellectually demanding and
do not enjoy tedious routines.

In relationships, you anger quickly if faced with stupidity or
deception, though you are just as quick to forgive and forget.
Emotionally, there are times when your heart rules your head.

Moon in Capricorn

The Moon in Capricorn makes you popular and likely to come into the public eye in some way. The watery Moon is not entirely comfortable in the Earth sign of Capricorn and this may lead to some difficulties in the early years of life. An initial lack of creative ability and indecision must be overcome before the true qualities of patience and perseverance inherent in Capricorn can show through.

You have good administrative ability and are a capable worker, and if you are careful you can accumulate wealth. But you must be cautious and take professional advice in partnerships, as you are open to deception. You may be interested in social or welfare work, which suit your organisational skills and sympathy for others.

Moon in Aquarius

The Moon in Aquarius makes you an active and agreeable person with a friendly, easy-going nature. Sympathetic to the needs of others, you flourish in a laid-back atmosphere. You are broad-minded, fair and open to suggestion, although sometimes you have an unconventional quality which others can find hard to understand.

You are interested in the strange and curious, and in old articles and places. You enjoy trips to these places and gain much from them. Political, scientific and educational work interests you and you might choose a career in science or technology.

Money-wise, you make gains through innovation and concentration and Lunar Aquarians often tackle more than one job at a time. In love you are kind and honest.

Moon in Pisces

You have a kind, sympathetic nature, somewhat retiring at times, but you always take account of others' feelings and help when you can.

Personal relationships may be problematic, but as life goes on you can learn from your experiences and develop a better understanding of yourself and the world around you.

You have a fondness for travel, appreciate beauty and harmony and hate disorder and strife. You may be fond of literature and would make a good writer or speaker yourself. You have a creative imagination and may come across as an incurable romantic. You have strong intuition, maybe bordering on a mediumistic quality, which sets you apart from the mass. You may not be rich in cash terms, but your personal gifts are worth more than gold.

LIBRA IN LOVE

Discover how compatible you are with people from the same and other signs of the zodiac. Five stars equals a match made in heaven!

Libra meets Libra

This is a potentially successful match because Librans are extremely likeable people, and so it stands to reason that two Librans together will be twice as pleasant and twice as much fun. However, Librans can also be indecisive and need an anchor from which to find practical and financial success, and obviously one Libran won't provide this for another. Librans can be flighty in a romantic sense, so both parties will need to develop a steadfast approach for a long-term relationship. Star rating: ****

Libra meets Scorpio

Many astrologers have reservations about this match because, on the surface, the signs are so different. However, this couple may find fulfilment because these differences mean that their respective needs are met. Scorpio needs a partner to lighten the load which won't daunt Libra, while Libra looks for a steadfast quality which it doesn't possess, but Scorpio can supply naturally. Financial success is possible because they both have good ideas and back them up with hard work and determination. All in all, a promising outlook. Star rating: ****

Libra meets Sagittarius

Libra and Sagittarius are both adaptable signs who get on well with most people, but this promising outlook often does not follow through because each brings out the flighty side of the other. This combination is great for a fling, but when the romance is over someone needs to see to the practical side of life. Both signs are well meaning, pleasant and kind, but are either of them constant enough to build a life together? In at least some of the cases, the answer would be no. Star rating: ***

Libra meets Capricorn

Libra and Capricorn rub each other up the wrong way because their attitudes to life are so different, and although both are capable of doing something about this, in reality they probably won't. Capricorn is steady, determined and solid, while Libra is bright but sometimes superficial and not entirely reliable. They usually lack the instant spark needed to get them together in the first place, so when it does happen it is often because one of the partners is not typical of their sign. Star rating: **

Libra meets Aquarius

One of the best combinations imaginable, partly because both are Air signs and so share a common meeting point. But perhaps the more crucial factor is that both signs respect each other. Aquarius loves life and originality, and is quite intellectual. Libra is similar, but more balanced and rather less eccentric. A visit to this couple's house would be entertaining and full of zany wit, activity and excitement. Both are keen to travel and may prefer to 'find themselves' before taking on too many domestic responsibilities. Star rating: *****

Libra meets Pisces

Libra and Pisces can be extremely fond of each other, even deeply in love, but this alone isn't a stable foundation for long-term success. Pisces is extremely deep and doesn't even know itself very well. Libra may initially find this intriguing but will eventually feel frustrated at being unable to understand the Piscean's emotional and personal feelings. Pisces can be jealous and may find Libra's flightiness difficult, which Libra can't stand. They are great friends and they may make it to the romantic stakes, but when they get there a lot of effort will be necessary. Star rating: ***

Libra meets Aries

These are zodiac opposites which means a make-or-break situation.
The match will either be a great success or a dismal failure. Why?
Well, Aries finds it difficult to understand the flighty Air-sign
tendencies of Libra, whilst the natural balance of Libra contradicts
the unorthodox Arian methods. Any flexibility will come from
Libra, which may mean that things work out for a while, but Libra
only has so much patience and it may eventually run out. In the end,
Aries may be just too bossy for an independent but sensitive sign like
Libra. Star rating: **

Libra meets Taurus

A happy life is important to both these signs and, as they are both
ruled by Venus, they share a common understanding, even though
they display themselves so differently. Taurus is quieter than Libra,
but can be decisive, and that's what counts. Libra is interested in
absolutely everything, an infectious quality when seen through
Taurean eyes. The slightly flighty qualities of Libra may lead to
jealousy from the Bull. Not an argumentative relationship and one
that often works well. There could be many changes of address for
this pair. Star rating: ****

Libra meets Gemini

One of the best possible zodiac combinations. Libra and Gemini are
both Air signs, which leads to a meeting of minds. Both signs simply
love to have a good time, although Libra is the tidiest and less
forgetful. Gemini's capricious nature won't bother Libra, who acts
as a stabilising influence. Life should generally run smoothly, and
any rows are likely to be short and sharp. Both parties genuinely like
each other, which is of paramount importance in a relationship and,
ultimately, there isn't a better reason for being or staying together.
Star rating: *****

Libra meets Cancer

Almost anyone can get on with Libra, which is one of the most adaptable signs of them all. But being adaptable does not always lead to fulfilment and a successful match here will require a quiet Libran and a slightly more progressive Cancerian than the norm. Both signs are pleasant and polite, and like domestic order, but Libra may find Cancer too emotional and perhaps lacking in vibrancy, while Libra, on the other hand, may be a little too flighty for steady Cancer. Star rating: ***

Libra meets Leo

The biggest drawback here is likely to be in the issue of commitment. Leo knows everything about constancy and faithfulness, a lesson which, sadly, Libra needs to learn. Librans are easy-going and diplomatic, qualities which are useful when Leo is on the war-path. This couple should be compatible on a personal level and any problems tend to relate to the different way in which these signs deal with outside factors. With good will and an open mind, it can work out well enough. Star rating: ***

Libra meets Virgo

There have been some rare occasions when this match has found great success, but usually the darker and more inward-looking Virgoan depresses the naturally gregarious Libran. Libra appears self-confident, but is not so beneath the surface, and needs encouragement to develop inner confidence, which may not come from Virgo. Constancy can be a problem for Libra, who also tires easily and may find Virgo dull. A lighter, less serious approach to life from Virgo is needed to make this work. Star rating: **

VENUS:
THE PLANET OF LOVE

If you look up at the sky around sunset or sunrise you will often see Venus in close attendance to the Sun. It is arguably one of the most beautiful sights of all and there is little wonder that historically it became associated with the goddess of love. But although Venus does play an important part in the way you view love and in the way others see you romantically, this is only one of the spheres of influence that it enjoys in your overall character.

Venus has a part to play in the more cultured side of your life and has much to do with your appreciation of art, literature, music and general creativity. Even the way you look is responsive to the part of the zodiac that Venus occupied at the start of your life, though this fact is also down to your Sun sign and Ascending sign. If, at the time you were born, Venus occupied one of the more gregarious zodiac signs, you will be more likely to wear your heart on your sleeve, as well as to be more attracted to entertainment, social gatherings and good company. If on the other hand Venus occupied a quiet zodiac sign at the time of your birth, you would tend to be more retiring and less willing to shine in public situations.

It's good to know what part the planet Venus plays in your life for it can have a great bearing on the way you appear to the rest of the world and since we all have to mix with others, you can learn to make the very best of what Venus has to offer you.

One of the great complications in the past has always been trying to establish exactly what zodiac position Venus enjoyed when you were born because the planet is notoriously difficult to track. However, we have solved that problem by creating a table that is exclusive to your Sun sign, which you will find on the following page.

Establishing your Venus sign could not be easier. Just look up the year of your birth on the next page and you will see a sign of the zodiac. This was the sign that Venus occupied in the period covered by your sign in that year. If Venus occupied more than one sign during the period, this is indicated by the date on which the sign changed, and the name of the new sign. For instance, if you were born in 1950, Venus was in Virgo until the 4th October, after which time it was in Libra. If you were born before 4th October your Venus sign is Virgo, if you were born on or after 4th October, your Venus sign is Libra. Once you have established the position of Venus at the time of your birth, you can then look in the pages which follow to see how this has a bearing on your life as a whole.

1919 SCORPIO / 12.10 SAGITTARIUS
1920 LIBRA / 30.9 SCORPIO
1921 LEO / 26.9 VIRGO /
    21.10 LIBRA
1922 SCORPIO / 11.10 SAGITTARIUS
1923 LIBRA / 16.10 SCORPIO
1924 LEO / 8.10 VIRGO
1925 SCORPIO / 12.10 SAGITTARIUS
1926 VIRGO / 6.10 LIBRA
1927 VIRGO
1928 LIBRA / 29.9 SCORPIO
1929 LEO / 26.9 VIRGO /
    20.10 LIBRA
1930 SCORPIO / 12.10 SAGITTARIUS
1931 LIBRA / 15.10 SCORPIO
1932 LEO / 7.10 VIRGO
1933 SCORPIO / 11.10 SAGITTARIUS
1934 VIRGO / 5.10 LIBRA
1935 VIRGO
1936 LIBRA / 28.9 SCORPIO
1937 LEO / 25.9 VIRGO /
    20.10 LIBRA
1938 SCORPIO / 14.10 SAGITTARIUS
1939 LIBRA / 14.10 SCORPIO
1940 LEO / 7.10 VIRGO
1941 SCORPIO / 11.10 SAGITTARIUS
1942 VIRGO / 5.10 LIBRA
1943 VIRGO
1944 LIBRA / 28.9 SCORPIO
1945 LEO / 25.9 VIRGO /
    19.10 LIBRA
1946 SCORPIO / 14.10 SAGITTARIUS
1947 LIBRA / 13.10 SCORPIO
1948 LEO / 7.10 VIRGO
1949 SCORPIO / 11.10 SAGITTARIUS
1950 VIRGO / 4.10 LIBRA
1951 VIRGO
1952 LIBRA / 27.9 SCORPIO
1953 VIRGO / 19.10 LIBRA
1954 SCORPIO / 16.10 SAGITTARIUS
1955 LIBRA / 12.10 SCORPIO
1956 LEO / 6.10 VIRGO
1957 SCORPIO / 10.10 SAGITTARIUS
1958 VIRGO / 4.10 LIBRA
1959 VIRGO / 28.9 LEO
1960 LIBRA / 27.9 SCORPIO
1961 VIRGO / 18.10 LIBRA
1962 SCORPIO / 16.10 SAGITTARIUS
1963 LIBRA / 12.10 SCORPIO
1964 LEO / 6.10 VIRGO
1965 SCORPIO / 9.10 SAGITTARIUS
1966 VIRGO / 4.10 LIBRA
1967 VIRGO / 3.10 LEO
1968 LIBRA / 26.9 SCORPIO

1969 VIRGO / 17.10 LIBRA
1970 SCORPIO / 19.10 SAGITTARIUS
1971 LIBRA / 11.10 SCORPIO
1972 LEO / 6.10 VIRGO
1973 SCORPIO / 9.10 SAGITTARIUS
1974 VIRGO / 3.10 LIBRA
1975 VIRGO / 5.10 LEO
1976 LIBRA / 26.9 SCORPIO
1977 VIRGO / 17.10 LIBRA
1978 SCORPIO / 19.10 SAGITTARIUS
1979 LIBRA / 11.10 SCORPIO
1980 LEO / 5.10 VIRGO
1981 SCORPIO / 9.10 SAGITTARIUS
1982 VIRGO / 3.10 LIBRA
1983 VIRGO / 7.10 LEO
1984 LIBRA / 25.9 SCORPIO
1985 VIRGO / 16.10 LIBRA
1986 SCORPIO
1987 LIBRA / 10.10 SCORPIO
1988 LEO / 5.10 VIRGO
1989 SCORPIO / 8.10 SAGITTARIUS
1990 VIRGO / 2.10 LIBRA
1991 VIRGO / 8.10 LEO
1992 LIBRA / 25.9 SCORPIO
1993 VIRGO / 16.10 LIBRA
1994 SCORPIO
1995 LIBRA / 10.10 SCORPIO
1996 LEO / 5.10 VIRGO
1997 SCORPIO / 8.10 SAGITTARIUS
1998 VIRGO / 2.10 LIBRA
1999 VIRGO / 9.10 LEO
2000 LIBRA / 25.9 SCORPIO
2001 LEO / 5.10 VIRGO
2002 SCORPIO / 8.10 SAGITTARIUS
2003 LIBRA / 10.10 SCORPIO
2004 LEO / 5.10 VIRGO
2005 SCORPIO / 8.10 SAGITTARIUS
2006 VIRGO / 2.10 LIBRA
2007 VIRGO / 9.10 LEO
2008 LIBRA / 25.9 SCORPIO
2009 LEO / 5.10 VIRGO
2010 SCORPIO / 8.10 SAGITTARIUS
2011 LIBRA / 10.10 SCORPIO
2012 LEO / 5.10 VIRGO
2013 SCORPIO / 8.10 SAGITTARIUS
2014 VIRGO / 2.10 LIBRA
2015 VIRGO / 9.10 LEO
2016 SCORPIO / 19.10 SAGITTARIUS
2017 LEO / 5.10 VIRGO

VENUS THROUGH THE ZODIAC SIGNS

Venus in Aries

Amongst other things, the position of Venus in Aries indicates a fondness for travel, music and all creative pursuits. Your nature tends to be affectionate and you would try not to create confusion or difficulty for others if it could be avoided. Many people with this planetary position have a great love of the theatre, and mental stimulation is of the greatest importance. Early romantic attachments are common with Venus in Aries, so it is very important to establish a genuine sense of romantic continuity. Early marriage is not recommended, especially if it is based on sympathy. You may give your heart a little too readily on occasions.

Venus in Taurus

You are capable of very deep feelings and your emotions tend to last for a very long time. This makes you a trusting partner and lover, whose constancy is second to none. In life you are precise and careful and always try to do things the right way. Although this means an ordered life, which you are comfortable with, it can also lead you to be rather too fussy for your own good. Despite your pleasant nature, you are very fixed in your opinions and quite able to speak your mind. Others are attracted to you and historical astrologers always quoted this position of Venus as being very fortunate in terms of marriage. However, if you find yourself involved in a failed relationship, it could take you a long time to trust again.

Venus in Gemini

As with all associations related to Gemini, you tend to be quite versatile, anxious for change and intelligent in your dealings with the world at large. You may gain money from more than one source but you are equally good at spending it. There is an inference here that you are a good communicator, via either the written or the spoken word, and you love to be in the company of interesting people. Always on the look-out for culture, you may also be very fond of music, and love to indulge the curious and cultured side of your nature. In romance you tend to have more than one relationship and could find yourself associated with someone who has previously been a friend or even a distant relative.

Venus in Cancer

You often stay close to home because you are very fond of family and enjoy many of your most treasured moments when you are with those you love. Being naturally sympathetic, you will always do anything you can to support those around you, even people you hardly know at all. This charitable side of your nature is your most noticeable trait and is one of the reasons why others are naturally so fond of you. Being receptive and in some cases even psychic, you can see through to the soul of most of those with whom you come into contact. You may not commence too many romantic attachments but when you do give your heart, it tends to be unconditionally.

Venus in Leo

It must become quickly obvious to almost anyone you meet that you are kind, sympathetic and yet determined enough to stand up for anyone or anything that is truly important to you. Bright and sunny, you warm the world with your natural enthusiasm and would rarely do anything to hurt those around you, or at least not intentionally. In romance you are ardent and sincere, though some may find your style just a little overpowering. Gains come through your contacts with other people and this could be especially true with regard to romance, for love and money often come hand in hand for those who were born with Venus in Leo. People claim to understand you, though you are more complex than you seem.

Venus in Virgo

Your nature could well be fairly quiet no matter what your Sun sign might be, though this fact often manifests itself as an inner peace and would not prevent you from being basically sociable. Some delays and even the odd disappointment in love cannot be ruled out with this planetary position, though it's a fact that you will usually find the happiness you look for in the end. Catapulting yourself into romantic entanglements that you know to be rather ill-advised is not sensible, and it would be better to wait before you committed yourself exclusively to any one person. It is the essence of your nature to serve the world at large and through doing so it is possible that you will attract money at some stage in your life.

Venus in Libra

Venus is very comfortable in Libra and bestows upon those people who have this planetary position a particular sort of kindness that is easy to recognise. This is a very good position for all sorts of friendships and also for romantic attachments that usually bring much joy into your life. Few individuals with Venus in Libra would avoid marriage and since you are capable of great depths of love, it is likely that you will find a contented personal life. You like to mix with people of integrity and intelligence but don't take kindly to scruffy surroundings or work that means getting your hands too dirty. Careful speculation, good business dealings and money through marriage all seem fairly likely.

Venus in Scorpio

You are quite open and tend to spend money quite freely, even on those occasions when you don't have very much. Although your intentions are always good, there are times when you get yourself in to the odd scrape and this can be particularly true when it comes to romance, which you may come to late or from a rather unexpected direction. Certainly you have the power to be happy and to make others contented on the way, but you find the odd stumbling block on your journey through life and it could seem that you have to work harder than those around you. As a result of this, you gain a much deeper understanding of the true value of personal happiness than many people ever do, and are likely to achieve true contentment in the end.

Venus in Sagittarius

You are lighthearted, cheerful and always able to see the funny side of any situation. These facts enhance your popularity, which is especially high with members of the opposite sex. You should never have to look too far to find romantic interest in your life, though it is just possible that you might be too willing to commit yourself before you are certain that the person in question is right for you. Part of the problem here extends to other areas of life too. The fact is that you like variety in everything and so can tire of situations that fail to offer it. All the same, if you choose wisely and learn to understand your restless side, then great happiness can be yours.

Venus in Capricorn

The most notable trait that comes from Venus in this position is that it makes you trustworthy and able to take on all sorts of responsibilities in life. People are instinctively fond of you and love you all the more because you are always ready to help those who are in any form of need. Social and business popularity can be yours and there is a magnetic quality to your nature that is particularly attractive in a romantic sense. Anyone who wants a partner for a lover, a spouse and a good friend too would almost certainly look in your direction. Constancy is the hallmark of your nature and unfaithfulness would go right against the grain. You might sometimes be a little too trusting.

Venus in Aquarius

This location of Venus offers a fondness for travel and a desire to try out something new at every possible opportunity. You are extremely easy to get along with and tend to have many friends from varied backgrounds, classes and inclinations. You like to live a distinct sort of life and gain a great deal from moving about, both in a career sense and with regard to your home. It is not out of the question that you could form a romantic attachment to someone who comes from far away or be attracted to a person of a distinctly artistic and original nature. What you cannot stand is jealousy, for you have friends of both sexes and would want to keep things that way.

Venus in Pisces

The first thing people tend to notice about you is your wonderful, warm smile. Being very charitable by nature you will do anything to help others, even if you don't know them well. Much of your life may be spent sorting out situations for other people, but it is very important to feel that you are living for yourself too. In the main, you remain cheerful, and tend to be quite attractive to members of the opposite sex. Where romantic attachments are concerned, you could be drawn to people who are significantly older or younger than yourself or to someone with a unique career or point of view. It might be best for you to avoid marrying whilst you are still very young.

LIBRA:
2016 DIARY PAGES

October 2016

1 SATURDAY
Moon Age Day 1   Moon Sign Libra

Your attitude to life in general may be shaped by a little offering from Lady Luck. You are very much inclined to trust your own judgement, which is sound at present. Concentrate on having a good time, even when you are undertaking jobs that might sometimes prove to be either distracting or difficult.

2 SUNDAY
Moon Age Day 2   Moon Sign Libra

Planetary benefits come along from a number of different directions whilst the lunar high is present. You can afford to back your hunches and might find yourself sought out by someone you think of as being extremely special. Although the summer is now definitely gone you may decide to spend time out of doors.

3 MONDAY
Moon Age Day 3   Moon Sign Scorpio

You may need the bright lights of the social world to cheer you up today. There are a number of astrological explanations for why you are feeling slightly down in the dumps, though there is no real reason to let these spoil your day. Keep in the mainstream at work and avoid unnecessary controversy.

4 TUESDAY
Moon Age Day 4   Moon Sign Scorpio

Stay away from speculation of any kind today and particularly so before the middle of the day. By this afternoon, it will appear that the reaction you get from others is more positive. This isn't really the case, it is merely that you begin to be less negative – feelings you have tended to project on to the world at large since yesterday.

5 WEDNESDAY   *Moon Age Day 5   Moon Sign Scorpio*

Life can prove very fulfilling at the moment, mainly as a result of the emotional support coming to you from the direction of loved ones. Making real progress in your work won't be too easy but it is far from certain you will actually care very much about this fact – at least until the end of the week.

6 THURSDAY   *Moon Age Day 6   Moon Sign Sagittarius*

The best advice that can be offered to Libra today is to ensure that you get one task out of the way before you start on another. There is a danger of overlap and confusion that you could so easily avoid. There ought to be a good deal of happiness about in a family and friendship sense.

7 FRIDAY   *Moon Age Day 7   Moon Sign Sagittarius*

All joint financial matters are especially well-starred at present, likewise monetary or business partnerships. In addition, you should find it easier to whisper those intimate little words that can make all the difference in the relationship stakes. Don't be too quick to jump to conclusions in the workplace.

8 SATURDAY   *Moon Age Day 8   Moon Sign Capricorn*

Improved communication is likely to be the best gift of the weekend. Don't be tardy when it comes to expressing an opinion, even when you know there are people around who will not agree with you. Although you won't be feeling absolutely positive about everything, you may be able to fool others and even yourself in the end.

9 SUNDAY   *Moon Age Day 9   Moon Sign Capricorn*

There are certain signposts to success around now, even if you have to keep your eyes wide open in order to recognise them. Socially speaking, you are anxious to meet new people and may well give some of your associations from the past the order of the boot. Libra is all about change and diversity at present.

10 MONDAY *Moon Age Day 10   Moon Sign Capricorn*

You could find the opinions of others to be either irrelevant of downright annoying now. It is important not to react too strongly so keep your cool. It is possible for you to score some singular successes, simply by refusing to rise to any bait that is presently offered.

11 TUESDAY *Moon Age Day 11   Moon Sign Aquarius*

Career matters should now be looking good. If you are in full time education, expect some good marks and compliments from tutors. Home-based activities could be slightly less than appealing, though you might have to turn your mind in that direction, if only to please your loved ones.

12 WEDNESDAY *Moon Age Day 12   Moon Sign Aquarius*

Your mind seems to be in sharp focus, to the extent that you feel you can see even the most distant horizon in your life. Look out for a little frustration arising from people who do things without checking, which could lead to a few problems for you further down the line.

13 THURSDAY *Moon Age Day 13   Moon Sign Pisces*

Don't be dissuaded from doing things your own way. If you put yourself out too much to accommodate the ideas of others, no matter how close they may be, you could be in for a loss of some sort. When your intuition tells you to take a specific course of action, it would be sensible to heed it.

14 FRIDAY *Moon Age Day 14   Moon Sign Pisces*

The potential for getting what you want across the board is strong today. There are people around who actively want to offer you help and support and you should be able to locate them easily enough. Conforming to the expectations that older relatives have of you could be somewhat complicated.

15 SATURDAY   *Moon Age Day 15   Moon Sign Aries*

If anything, you are being slightly less consistent today, a good indication that you are not firing on all cylinders. Perhaps you need to look at certain matters with greater care and it would help to keep quiet about them until you have. There are gains to be made, though you will have to look hard to find them.

16 SUNDAY   *Moon Age Day 16   Moon Sign Aries*

Once again, you are quiet and contemplative. Although you won't personally see this as being a problem, people who have great expectations of you might. It should not be particularly difficult to explain yourself and in any case, by tomorrow afternoon the Moon will have moved on, taking this mood with it. Delaying tactics are called for.

17 MONDAY   *Moon Age Day 17   Moon Sign Taurus*

Emotional issues and the way you view them are inclined to dominate personal relationships at present whereas practical matters should be taking centre stage. If you can, defuse issues before they take on any real importance and avoid getting involved in discussions you know could be contentious.

18 TUESDAY   *Moon Age Day 18   Moon Sign Taurus*

There is plenty of initiative available for professional developments, though simple friendship might be taking something of a back seat at this stage of the week. This may be the case because you are so busy with other matters. Exercise some caution in financial affairs.

19 WEDNESDAY   *Moon Age Day 19   Moon Sign Gemini*

You can attract just the right sort of company today, which means getting on in life, something that is of great importance to you whilst the Sun occupies its present position in your chart. If there isn't all that much time for pleasantries today, you are at least showing kindness and compassion.

20 THURSDAY   *Moon Age Day 20   Moon Sign Gemini*

Most Libran people would be quite happy to take a break right now. It has been a busy and in some ways demanding period, without the number of social and personal diversions you need. Some respite comes today and you will certainly want to make the most of all opportunities to find a change of scene.

21 FRIDAY   *Moon Age Day 21   Moon Sign Cancer*

You are ready for almost any challenge life can throw at you, plus a few you invent for yourself. All the same, you don't have to go looking for imaginary enemies just in order to get some excitement into your life. If you haven't enough to do, there are people close at hand, who would welcome some help from you.

22 SATURDAY   *Moon Age Day 22   Moon Sign Cancer*

In money matters, your present ability to think quickly is going to prove extremely useful. Although you are unlikely to be gambling in the generally accepted sense of the word, you are willing to take a chance that could lead to greater monetary strength further down the line. Make time to enjoy yourself later in the day.

23 SUNDAY   *Moon Age Day 23   Moon Sign Leo*

There may not be time to do everything you had planned today, but you will be determined to at least have a try. Confidence remains essentially high, particularly when you are dealing with subject matter that is familiar to you. Your creative potential is especially strong and shows itself in all facets of life.

24 MONDAY   *Moon Age Day 24   Moon Sign Leo*

The challenge today is to keep one step ahead of the competition. This is as true at work as it is in more social or sporting situations. Not everyone you know proves to be adept at expressing either their opinions or wishes today. This leads to a good deal of second-guessing as far as you are concerned.

25 TUESDAY *Moon Age Day 25   Moon Sign Leo*

There are new highlights in love and romance, which might come as something of a shock to a few Librans, who have placed such considerations firmly on the back burner during the last couple of weeks. If you feel at all lethargic today, the secret is to pitch in early in the day and to boost your sense of achievement.

26 WEDNESDAY *Moon Age Day 26   Moon Sign Virgo*

Current planetary trends have the ability to bring out the best in you and they help to make life supportive and stable – which is fine right now. You should feel generally comfortable at home and might not exhibit that need for movement that has been so much a part of your nature during the last few weeks.

27 THURSDAY *Moon Age Day 27   Moon Sign Virgo*

Financial consolidation is on your mind and you could be looking at family money very closely indeed. Don't be fooled into making any purchase that you know is flippant or unnecessary. Keep a cool head in a minor crisis and you will soon be laughing at the whole situation.

28 FRIDAY *Moon Age Day 28   Moon Sign Libra*

Now you can speed ahead and make more genuine progress in your life than has been possible for some days, despite the apparent movement that has taken place in your life. The difference now is that you are more considered in your attitude and you are integrating relationships and practical matters much better.

29 SATURDAY *Moon Age Day 29   Moon Sign Libra*

The lunar high does much to redress a few balances now and finds you more centred in your attitude. Contacts with others are less strained and you show strong diplomatic skills, which are the province of your zodiac sign. When it comes to money, you can afford to chance your arm at the moment.

30 SUNDAY
Moon Age Day 0   Moon Sign Libra

The planetary focus today is on your presently strong personality and the way others view it. Even those you mix with frequently are not used to seeing the very determined Libra, so give them the odd smile or wink to let them know you haven't really changed at all. Nevertheless, remain specific in your intentions.

31 MONDAY
Moon Age Day 1   Moon Sign Scorpio

You could find a degree of restlessness pervading your life as October draws to its close. You need something different to do and maybe some alternative people to share the situation with you. The week ahead can be quite interesting but it all really depends on just how much effort you are willing to put in.

♎ November 2016

1 TUESDAY
Moon Age Day 2   Moon Sign Scorpio

The emphasis today is on life's more playful aspects. Taking anything particularly seriously is going to be hard, at least until after Wednesday. However, your offbeat sense of humour and off-the-wall attitude will be popular with almost everyone and can actually see you achieving a great deal.

2 WEDNESDAY
Moon Age Day 3   Moon Sign Sagittarius

There ought to be pleasure coming from anything that means getting out of a rut. You won't take kindly to being tied down at the moment and will function better if you have room to breathe and to move. Even casual conversations can have quite far-reaching and positive implications.

3 THURSDAY
Moon Age Day 4   Moon Sign Sagittarius

Your attention may be called to specific hitches that come along this Thursday. Maybe arrangements you have made don't come off or you could have to reorganise things at the last minute. Family members might not be especially helpful at a time when you could do with some positive input.

4 FRIDAY
Moon Age Day 5   Moon Sign Sagittarius

It looks as though professional matters are well starred at the moment, even if it doesn't seem to be that way at first. When you are faced with awkward people today, turn on that natural charm and watch situations change quickly. You might have to show a good deal of give and take in romantic attachments.

5 SATURDAY   *Moon Age Day 6   Moon Sign Capricorn*

You could be rather socially reluctant today, which might not appear to bode well for the weekend. This probably isn't the case. You are likely to be very good when mixing with people you know well and only demonstrate a degree of reserve when having to deal with those who are virtual strangers.

6 SUNDAY   *Moon Age Day 7   Moon Sign Capricorn*

Be careful when it comes to listening to gossip. There is a good chance that much of what you hear today is either misleading or downright wrong. Opt for some fresh air if you can. This is Sunday after all and locking yourself in the house won't be good for you, mentally or physically.

7 MONDAY   *Moon Age Day 8   Moon Sign Aquarius*

Find something new and interesting with which you can start the week. The more entertaining you find life to be, the better you are likely to deal with it. Also, stand by to enter a new period in terms of relationships during which the motives of others become easier to understand.

8 TUESDAY   *Moon Age Day 9   Moon Sign Aquarius*

Your charming and playful side is now clearly on display. Don't be too distracted by the fun and games that are available because there is plenty for you to do in a practical sense. Many Librans are now looking at the possibility of making changes to their living environments.

9 WEDNESDAY   *Moon Age Day 10   Moon Sign Pisces*

Challenges are likely, as are confrontations because now you are not half so willing to sit back and watch others lord it over you. On the contrary, you are not only competitive at present but also probably more than willing to defend yourself before you have even been attacked. Learn how to count to ten.

10 THURSDAY

Moon Age Day 11   Moon Sign Pisces

The focus now shifts to the social arena. If there are any invitations on offer today, grab them with both hands. You need the support of friends and relatives if you are going to get the very best out of any given situation. What you don't need is to be nagged, so stay away from people who insist on moaning about anything.

11 FRIDAY

Moon Age Day 12   Moon Sign Pisces

The instinct for skilful money-making is strong at the moment. There are ways and means to bring more cash into your life and you will recognise most of them. Although you could be finding the going a little tough in terms of casual friendships, the people who love you the most won't let you down.

12 SATURDAY

Moon Age Day 13   Moon Sign Aries

There is a temporary lull beginning today. You don't want it and will fight against it but facts are facts. What you can do very well at the moment is to think. Looking ahead, making plans and getting yourself into a more favourable position generally is going to be both important and relevant.

13 SUNDAY

Moon Age Day 14   Moon Sign Aries

The fewer mistakes you make today, the better you are going to feel about life as a whole. Concentration may not be easy but you will win through if you simply employ a degree of dogged determination. Don't necessarily expect a high degree of co-operation, even from people who usually lend a hand.

14 MONDAY

Moon Age Day 15   Moon Sign Taurus

This is a day during which you will want to speed ahead. Obstacles placed in your path can be avoided because it won't do you much good to face them head-on at present. If one person doesn't like what you have to say, find someone else. Perseverance and determination can work wonders.

15 TUESDAY   *Moon Age Day 16   Moon Sign Taurus*

It appears that you are on the lookout for new acquaintances. If this means you have become somewhat bored with your usual social crowd, think about a new interest or pastime that you would find stimulating. You need to keep those grey cells working and cannot stand feeling bored.

16 WEDNESDAY   *Moon Age Day 17   Moon Sign Gemini*

The further you are able to go today, the better you will feel. This is true in terms of journeys you might choose to take, but also with regard to issues that you are likely to push beyond previous limits. Don't allow anyone or anything to hold you back during this most important interlude.

17 THURSDAY   *Moon Age Day 18   Moon Sign Gemini*

Professional matters can be a real labour of love today, which is just as well because they are not offering too much in the way of financial remuneration. Be patient, better monetary times are at hand but they are not here quite yet. All the same, be certain that you check your lottery ticket carefully if you have bought one today.

18 FRIDAY   *Moon Age Day 19   Moon Sign Cancer*

Don't listen to the tall tales of others today and at the same time be careful you are not spreading any gossip yourself. If you need to know something, it would be far better to check out the details for yourself. You are quite creative now and might be in the mood to turn out a delicious meal.

19 SATURDAY   *Moon Age Day 20   Moon Sign Cancer*

At the start of the weekend it might seem that you work much better in groups. Libra is a social animal at the best of times but much more so now. The only difficulty today would be if circumstances forced you to spend long periods of time relying on your own company.

20 SUNDAY
Moon Age Day 21   Moon Sign Leo

Work and professional matters should prove more than fulfilling. Even if you don't have to toil professionally on a Sunday, you will find something to keep you occupied. Physical activity is very good for you, as long as you don't do the usual air-sign trick and overdo it. Moderation in all things is the key.

21 MONDAY
Moon Age Day 22   Moon Sign Leo

You want to make a powerful impression on others today and it should not be too difficult to achieve that objective. Not too far off is the lunar high and it isn't too soon to start determining how you can use the extra energy that is coming your way. For the moment, you need to concentrate, especially at work.

22 TUESDAY
Moon Age Day 23   Moon Sign Virgo

As far as personal and emotional security are concerned, you should find yourself well looked after today. In terms of your nature, you are charming and well co-ordinated at the moment – with just the right attitude necessary to get on well in life. You also exude a sort of wisdom that others will recognise.

23 WEDNESDAY
Moon Age Day 24   Moon Sign Virgo

Confidence tends to be fairly high, even if action is somewhat subdued. You won't have long to wait for things to get moving again and in the meantime, you can enjoy watching life go by, rather than having to be at the front of every queue. Concern for family members could be great but is probably not justified.

24 THURSDAY
Moon Age Day 25   Moon Sign Libra

The lunar high finds you fighting fit and anxious to make the best sort of impression. If there is any fly in the ointment at all, it could be that not everyone you come across is equally helpful. Put your best foot forward at work but leave time for personal enjoyment coming your way later in the day.

25 FRIDAY
Moon Age Day 26   Moon Sign Libra

The go-ahead influence continues and you find people rather more willing to live with your suggestions now. Part of the reason is your persuasive tongue and you won't have much trouble bringing people round to your point of view. Romance is especially well-starred for those on the lookout for it.

26 SATURDAY
Moon Age Day 27   Moon Sign Libra

In practical matters, you need to keep your eye on the ball. This is not a time to diversify too much and concentration is all-important. If you feel that family members are not taking their own responsibilities quite as seriously as they should, this might be the right time to gently let them know.

27 SUNDAY
Moon Age Day 28   Moon Sign Scorpio

Today is a time for thinking about recent proposals and for following them to their logical conclusion. If you have recently embarked on something that could only really be called a labour of love, you may be about to discover that it can also be profitable. Spend part of your Sunday with family members.

28 MONDAY
Moon Age Day 29   Moon Sign Scorpio

Things that are happening at home help to redress the balance at work, where you are likely to be extremely active. Use some of your spare hours to quite simply have a rest and don't take on any more tasks than are strictly necessary at this time. Avoid getting on the wrong side of someone who is quite influential.

29 TUESDAY
Moon Age Day 0   Moon Sign Sagittarius

A combination of leisure and romance ought to appeal today, in those moments when you are not busy working. If you want to avoid becoming bored with routines, it would be sensible to deliberately make alterations to your regimes. There is little to worry about at the moment, though probably a shortage of excitement.

30 WEDNESDAY   *Moon Age Day 1   Moon Sign Sagittarius*

Now you find yourself well able to get your ideas across to others and to make the very best of impressions on the world at large. It is as if you have suddenly heard the starter's gun because you race ahead, particularly in practical matters. Romantically speaking, you ought to let someone know how you feel.

♎

December 2016

1 THURSDAY   *Moon Age Day 2   Moon Sign Sagittarius*

Encounters with people who come new into your life could prove to be something of an inspiration now. Someone, somewhere seeks to offer you some timely advice and it would be sensible to at least listen, even if you decide to follow your own path in any case. All in all, this should be a positive day.

2 FRIDAY   *Moon Age Day 3   Moon Sign Capricorn*

Simple conversation is what proves to be most useful today. The things you hear as you go about from place to place could inspire you in some way and might lead to ideas that can mature in the fullness of time. Although you can be of tremendous use to friends, there are some things you cannot do for them.

3 SATURDAY   *Moon Age Day 4   Moon Sign Capricorn*

Put all thoughts of work behind you if you are a Libran who has the weekend to yourself. Now comes a time when you can think specifically about romance and the social side of life. This might be just about the first time you have realised that Christmas is just around the corner.

4 SUNDAY   *Moon Age Day 5   Moon Sign Aquarius*

Although there are plenty of people around you at the moment, this is one of those days when you are inclined to make decisions more or less alone. This does not mean locking yourself away in a darkened room for hours at a stretch but present trends do indicate that you will not be susceptible to the influence of others.

5 MONDAY   *Moon Age Day 6   Moon Sign Aquarius*

This is likely to be a day of busy demands and keenly-felt responsibilities. Getting those close to you to do what is expected of them may not be easy but is necessary to your own peace of mind. Try not to push yourself too hard, particularly since there appears to be no special reason for doing so.

6 TUESDAY   *Moon Age Day 7   Moon Sign Aquarius*

Gradually, you find yourself identifying more with the needs and aspirations of the group and that means that as the month wears on any recent solitary qualities are inclined to disappear. The quirky side of Libra begins to show more, though in ways that make your relatives and friends smile.

7 WEDNESDAY   *Moon Age Day 8   Moon Sign Pisces*

This should prove to be a really inspiring day in almost every respect. Mercury strengthens its position in your chart, inclining you to adopt a more sociable and tolerant attitude. This alone should make you feel more comfortable because it is the way Libra operates for most of the time.

8 THURSDAY   *Moon Age Day 9   Moon Sign Pisces*

Today marks a time when it would be wise to follow your instincts, which are unlikely to let you down. Although not everyone you meet at present is equally reliable, it ought to be fairly easy for you to sort out the wheat from the chaff. Turn up your intuition and listen carefully to what it is telling you.

9 FRIDAY   *Moon Age Day 10   Moon Sign Aries*

You may feel as if you are swimming against the tide as you struggle to reach goals and objectives you feel to be close to your heart. Try not to take life too seriously and realise that the period after the present lunar low will bring a host of alternatives and possibilities you haven't even had time to think about yet.

10 SATURDAY *Moon Age Day 11   Moon Sign Aries*

It isn't friends but more likely acquaintances that are the most important to you at the moment. Casual conversations can have great significance to your future. It is true that Libra is filled with good ideas at the moment, whilst the Christmas break might give you the time to look at some of them more closely.

11 SUNDAY *Moon Age Day 12   Moon Sign Taurus*

A general air of good luck is likely to remain in place for most of today. Right now you want to mix with as many people as you can, and you take great delight from meetings with individuals who have not played a significant role in your life previously. If the weather is bad, you may decide to stay mainly indoors.

12 MONDAY *Moon Age Day 13   Moon Sign Taurus*

Don't get concerned about slight reversals in terms of money. As long as you have your eye on the situation in a general sense, things should turn out fine in the end. Make tasks you have to undertake part of a logical process, starting at the beginning and working steadily through to their completion.

13 TUESDAY *Moon Age Day 14   Moon Sign Gemini*

The main area of fulfilment today should come through your family. Getting on positively in terms of your career is slightly more difficult, though any problems here are likely to be little more than a hiccup. Socially speaking, it appears that the festive season has started already for Libra.

14 WEDNESDAY *Moon Age Day 15   Moon Sign Gemini*

Your fun-loving nature is stimulated by present planetary trends and that means the joker inside you comes to the fore at almost every turn. Ignore any tendency to hold back in a particular situation, which may arise because you doubt the reaction of colleagues. You have things to say, and the world is quite willing to lend an ear.

15 THURSDAY   *Moon Age Day 16   Moon Sign Cancer*

You can look forward to an influx of bright new ideas and should expect to enjoy a positive reception from an admiring audience. Your usual ways of relaxing might not fit the bill at present and it is entirely possible that you will be looking for new alternatives to pep up your social hours, particularly this evening.

16 FRIDAY   *Moon Age Day 17   Moon Sign Cancer*

Beware of potential setbacks. These are not especially likely, as long as you are not over-confident in your approach. Rather than commence any new project today, wait until tomorrow and see how you feel about it by then. There's a good chance that by then you will have modified your strategy.

17 SATURDAY   *Moon Age Day 18   Moon Sign Leo*

You would move heaven and earth to make someone you care about happy, but even that might not be enough today. You can't be held responsible for everyone all of the time. As long as you bear this fact in mind, and yet still offer assistance when you can, you are doing everything that could be expected of a decent human being.

18 SUNDAY   *Moon Age Day 19   Moon Sign Leo*

The most interesting times today come when you are swapping stories and jokes with people you feel comfortable being around. Don't take anything too seriously at present and be quite willing to see the really funny side of life, which shows itself time and again throughout the day.

19 MONDAY   *Moon Age Day 20   Moon Sign Virgo*

When slightly risky situations arise, you can afford to back your intuition, which is extremely strong at the moment. It isn't like Libra to take great chances, but the ones around at present are calculated. Money matters should be better and you are keeping the necessities of Christmas well in view.

20 TUESDAY ☿ *Moon Age Day 21* *Moon Sign Virgo*

There can be fruitful encounters with a number of different individuals today, some of whom are offering the sort of information that is both timely and useful. Where love and romance are concerned, it is not difficult to find the right words to sweep someone off their feet.

21 WEDNESDAY ☿ *Moon Age Day 22* *Moon Sign Virgo*

You need to mix with as many different sorts of people today as proves to be possible. At the back of your mind are a number of different ideas, some of which involve innovation. There are individuals appearing now who will listen to what you have to say and who may even help you to push forward progressively.

22 THURSDAY ☿ *Moon Age Day 23* *Moon Sign Libra*

This is the best time during December for getting the maximum amount done in the shortest time possible. The lunar high finds you quite organised, though still inclined to go it alone more than would often be the case. Nevertheless, you do show a very positive face to the world on just about every level of your life.

23 FRIDAY ☿ *Moon Age Day 24* *Moon Sign Libra*

These last few days before Christmas will find you rushing around, trying to deal with those last minute details, whilst at the same time getting the very best from your social life. Intimate relationships are still especially well-starred and it looks as though you are going to have a very 'warm' Christmas.

24 SATURDAY ☿ *Moon Age Day 25* *Moon Sign Scorpio*

The planetary positions suggest that Christmas Eve will offer variety. Be prepared to go that extra mile for the sake of family members and don't forget to leave time during the evening to wrap up those few last presents. This ought to be a very social sort of day for Libra and one you can really enjoy.

25 SUNDAY ☿ *Moon Age Day 26* *Moon Sign Scorpio*

You should have plenty to keep you busy on Christmas Day, both inside the family and further afield. This is unlikely to be a totally stop-at-home sort of day for many Librans and a little excitement is quite possible. The only difficult aspect to today might be in responding to some expectations.

26 MONDAY ☿ *Moon Age Day 27* *Moon Sign Scorpio*

You can expect to be the centre of attention today, which is why it would be sensible to line up in your mind all those things you would wish others to do for you. It isn't selfish to make use of your popularity and, in any case, most of the people you encounter should be more than happy to oblige.

27 TUESDAY ☿ *Moon Age Day 28* *Moon Sign Sagittarius*

This is certainly likely to be a very positive time when it comes to pleasing family members and friends alike. All the same, you can consider this to be 'your' day during the Christmas break and a time when you can choose to do more or less what suits you. This might include spending at least some time alone.

28 WEDNESDAY ☿ *Moon Age Day 29* *Moon Sign Sagittarius*

Any sense of rush or urgency on your part today could well be misplaced. The fact is that you are getting on rather well with most aspects of life, even if some of them are not coming good quite as quickly as you might wish. Keep in mind the needs you know family members have of you, and especially those of your partner.

29 THURSDAY ☿ *Moon Age Day 0* *Moon Sign Capricorn*

Emotive issues in relationships take centre stage for some Libran subjects today. Don't be too ready to allow these a great deal of room in your mind. It is possible that you are not being anywhere near as rational as you usually are. It looks as though you need to take a longer-term view of situations.

30 FRIDAY ☿ *Moon Age Day 1   Moon Sign Capricorn*

Relatives and friends will find you to be talkative, inquisitive and extremely friendly at the moment. Your level of general good luck is high, so you can afford to go an extra step further than would normally be the case. Love and romance wait around the corner for Libra subjects who are actively seeking either.

31 SATURDAY ☿ *Moon Age Day 2   Moon Sign Capricorn*

Entertaining people at home ought to prove to be immensely satisfying at the moment, but you may discover that there isn't quite as much scope for romance as you may have wished. Exactly the right words to please your lover seem to be eluding you for the moment – but just wait until the end of that New Year party.

LIBRA:
2017 DIARY PAGES

LIBRA:
YOUR YEAR IN BRIEF

It's important to start the year as you mean to go on, even if you feel a little lacking in vitality as things get started. January and February bring positive trends and a desire to get ahead, no matter what the price. There are financial gains to be made and you have plenty of incentive to work at relationships. Rules and regulations may be irritating, but should not hinder your desire to keep pushing forward. Aries is good at beating the odds in any situation.

You are willing to do almost anything you can to help others and to take on board new challenges at every turn. This is particularly obvious in the earliest days of spring. March and April may bring some financial and professional success, but even this is partly due to the good offices of others, helped by your own attitude. Take a little care when it comes to expenditure and don't go further than is strictly sensible at this time.

May and June will find you really waking up to the advancing year. This is a time to make progress at work and also a period to make some surprising new friendships. You won't tolerate routines and you will be quite happy to ring the changes in your life whenever and wherever possible. Stand by for new responsibilities in May.

July and August are definitely months for love. Throughout both you will be looking at relationships in a new light and doing all you can to strengthen your commitment and prove how steadfast and reliable you can be. Take any opportunity to overthrow normal boundaries and allow your unique personality to shine through. Avoid family arguments at this time but don't always do what is strictly expected of you. Make plenty of time for travel, especially during August.

Both September and October have a great deal to offer in terms of variety. You still feel the need to ring the changes whenever possible and you will soon get bored if everything remains the same from day to day. The attitude of friends and in particular loved ones could be mystifying, so it's just as well your intuition is turned up to full at this time. Some financial gains are indicated during the middle and towards the end of October.

November is likely to be slow to start and may be frustrating at times, but things will soon start to liven up. By the end of the month you will be firing on all cylinders and anxious to make the best of impressions. December could be the most progressive month of the year and is good for love, financial gain and establishing new attachments in your life.

January 2017

1 SUNDAY
☿ *Moon Age Day 4* *Moon Sign Aquarius*

This would be a great time to rid yourself of old attachments that are no longer of any use to you. Note, though, that this trend relates more to people than possessions. Libra is inclined to make all sorts of attachments that really only slow you down in the end. A tidier and leaner sort of life would suit you better in 2017.

2 MONDAY
☿ *Moon Age Day 5* *Moon Sign Aquarius*

Material matters can be both difficult to deal with and rather expensive under present trends. If you stop and think about things you should soon realise that the most important gifts in your life at the moment don't cost anything at all. Be confident that friends will come good for you when it matters the most.

3 TUESDAY
☿ *Moon Age Day 6* *Moon Sign Pisces*

A quite significant risk may hold no fear for you now. This is because you are sure of yourself and the people who surround you inspire you with added confidence. Trends suggest that the chances of you being let down at this time are quite small so you can probably afford to enjoy this confidence.

4 WEDNESDAY
☿ *Moon Age Day 7* *Moon Sign Pisces*

At this time it is likely that you will react very favourably to the input of someone whose ideas and opinions you value greatly. You have a great desire for freedom and a need to understand not only what is going on around you, but why. Love might be put on the back burner as you focus on worldly matters.

5 THURSDAY ☿ *Moon Age Day 8   Moon Sign Aries*

This is certainly not your luckiest period of the month and neither will you be overflowing with energy and confidence. It would be best to allow others to take the strain, whilst you concentrate on thinking up your moves for the future. Despite the lunar low you can be quite content if you only adopt the right attitude.

6 FRIDAY ☿ *Moon Age Day 9   Moon Sign Aries*

Routines could become quite stifling, which is why you should take a break from them if you can. There are plenty of people around who would be more than willing to help you out so put on a positive face and accept their assistance. By the end of today everything should begin to look much clearer.

7 SATURDAY ☿ *Moon Age Day 10   Moon Sign Taurus*

You thrive on doing several different tasks at the same time under present planetary trends and won't have too much difficulty making sure that they are all done well. Saturday could bring new opportunities as far as your love life is concerned and you should find it easy to utter the right words of love that have someone special melting.

8 SUNDAY *Moon Age Day 11   Moon Sign Taurus*

The personal side of your life brings many more benefits at the moment than the practical world. There is time to talk and an ability on your part to understand the deepest and most intimate responses of those around you. Analysing the thoughts of others is presently like gazing through crystal clear water for you.

9 MONDAY *Moon Age Day 12   Moon Sign Gemini*

There may be conflicts of interest around at the moment which make it difficult to get what you personally want from life, whilst at the same time fulfilling what you see as your obligations towards others. Be careful when making new investments because something that looks like a real bargain could turn out to be anything but.

10 TUESDAY   *Moon Age Day 13   Moon Sign Gemini*

If you make sure you get out and about today you could meet people who will be of real use to you in the future, and others who simply interest you. Concentrating on the same old things is not to be recommended at this time and you will be far better off taking an overall view of things when possible.

11 WEDNESDAY   *Moon Age Day 14   Moon Sign Cancer*

Today should be favourable for intimate relationships and for pushing forward progressively in romantic attachments. Although you will still be working hard in a practical sense it is the deeper side of your mind that predominates. It should be easy to let someone know how you really feel about them.

12 THURSDAY   *Moon Age Day 15   Moon Sign Cancer*

You might be so preoccupied with personal or emotional issues right now that social possibilities are missed. If your partner is quiet or family members are reacting in a rather strange way, give them space and time. Meanwhile, mix with friends who make fewer demands of you. A light and breezy attitude now works best.

13 FRIDAY   *Moon Age Day 16   Moon Sign Cancer*

You seem to be on the up and up as far as professional matters are concerned, though this might not seem to be particularly important ahead of the weekend. At the same time you have a great need for change and diversity and should have little or no trouble making the best of impressions wherever you choose you put yourself.

14 SATURDAY   *Moon Age Day 17   Moon Sign Leo*

Travel to new and previously unexplored places this weekend and do everything you can to stimulate the deeper side of your nature. You are intelligent and shrewd but somewhat lacking in stimulation at the moment. The things that can come to you are clearly inspired by your own attitude and the arrangements you make now.

15 SUNDAY
Moon Age Day 18   Moon Sign Leo

It looks as though you might just underestimate your present strengths and that would be a shame. You are far stronger than you realise, both physically and mentally and you have such a good attitude to life at present that you can achieve almost anything. All that is required is greater self-belief, together with a little timely help.

16 MONDAY
Moon Age Day 19   Moon Sign Virgo

For Libra right now, romance has rarely been better. This would be an excellent time for going out and about with your partner, but also for getting on board with new schemes dreamed up by your friends. You should be in a sparkling frame of mind, which will redress the balance if those around you are less motivated.

17 TUESDAY
Moon Age Day 20   Moon Sign Virgo

In a contemplative mood today, there are gains to be made but these may be small. The Moon now passes through your solar twelfth house, which always happens just before it returns to your own zodiac sign. This would be an ideal day to get things organised, ahead of a big push that begins early tomorrow morning.

18 WEDNESDAY
Moon Age Day 21   Moon Sign Libra

This is the first day of your lunar high – that time each month when the Moon returns to your own zodiac sign. You can afford to push your luck a little and should notice that most of your efforts work out well, without much conscious effort on your part. Confidence remains generally high until the weekend.

19 THURSDAY
Moon Age Day 22   Moon Sign Libra

This is an ideal time to set out on a few new projects that have been at the back of your mind for a while. It should be very easy indeed to get others to do your bidding and there will be no lack of positive indications that you are going in the right direction. In a social sense the weekend is likely to begin a couple of days early.

20 FRIDAY
Moon Age Day 23   Moon Sign Scorpio

Your social life is likely to expand at this time and you may be seeking out new forms of entertainment. It is also possible that you want to expand your horizons somewhat and any form of educational process would be looked on favourably under present trends. General good luck is reasonably high but effort counts.

21 SATURDAY
Moon Age Day 24   Moon Sign Scorpio

Even everyday conversations can lead you in the direction of advancement and it also looks as though there may be a chance to get ahead in your work. Once again you will probably be taking on more responsibility and you may decide to look at the possibility of a change of job, or at the very least changes within your current work.

22 SUNDAY
Moon Age Day 25   Moon Sign Scorpio

This would be an excellent time to improve yourself in some way, even if this is merely inside your own head. Broader experiences would be good but you won't get these by sitting and waiting. Extra effort is necessary if you really want to shine and like the good Libran you are there is much planning taking place.

23 MONDAY
Moon Age Day 26   Moon Sign Sagittarius

Make every effort to get yourself out of doors, no matter what the weather may be doing. You need fresh air and exercise and will soon become lethargic if you stick around in front of the fire. With a new week ahead there are also new opportunities on the way. Many of these have a social aspect and will brighten your life.

24 TUESDAY
Moon Age Day 27   Moon Sign Sagittarius

A new interest involving outdoor pursuits is in the offing and it is vitally important that you get as much fresh air and exercise as possible at this time. Also make yourself open to new ideas and better prospects for your financial future. In between, you will still be happy to be part of an interesting group.

25 WEDNESDAY *Moon Age Day 28   Moon Sign Capricorn*

Talks and negotiations with interesting and stimulating people are meat and drink to you under present planetary trends. Make sure you are as truthful as possible because people really do want to know what you are thinking. Your normal way of dealing with colleagues or friends may not work so try to be as original as possible.

26 THURSDAY *Moon Age Day 29   Moon Sign Capricorn*

An expanded sense of optimism helps you to plough on with things regardless and you will be on top form when it comes to communicating with the world at large. You may make some successful and interesting contacts and there are ever newer and better ways to prove your worth. This may be the most optimistic phase of the month so far.

27 FRIDAY *Moon Age Day 0   Moon Sign Capricorn*

Look for a powerful period during which you might rethink your direction at work. Out there in the practical world there are jobs that need doing and you will want to get them done in your own way. Maybe this could lead to difficulties with others because it's almost certain that some people with disagree with your methods.

28 SATURDAY *Moon Age Day 1   Moon Sign Aquarius*

Family issues will turn out to be your best area this weekend and you may well be pleased to leave the cares of the working world alone for a couple of days. Under prevailing planetary trends you are apt to be more nostalgic and also quite committed to those you love. A homely sort of weekend could be on the cards.

29 SUNDAY *Moon Age Day 2   Moon Sign Aquarius*

Firm up your securities and spend some time looking at financial matters today. There are ways and means of getting more money, even if you have to be just a little duplicitous in the way you go about it. There are competitors around at the moment and you will have to deal with them as and when they arise today.

30 MONDAY   *Moon Age Day 3   Moon Sign Pisces*

You are facing a period where definite gains can be made if you seek out change and diversity on all levels of your life. This may be the first time this year when you lift your eyes to look at the practical side of things. At work others will rely on you heavily but the extra responsibility is unlikely to faze you at all.

31 TUESDAY   *Moon Age Day 4   Moon Sign Pisces*

Commitments at home are your main priority today, though these are trends that probably won't impinge too much on the working day. It's simply that your nearest and dearest will be on your mind and you may also be thinking up ways to give your partner some sort of surprise to let them know how much you care.

2017

1 WEDNESDAY
Moon Age Day 5   Moon Sign Aries

The Moon now moves into the zodiac sign of Aries, which is your opposite zodiac sign. This brings that time of the month known as the lunar low and it is generally a period when you withdraw into yourself more than usual. This could make you quiet, which may cause others some concern. Assure them that you are fine.

2 THURSDAY
Moon Age Day 6   Moon Sign Aries

There could be a strong sense that some goals are not worth pursuing but much depends on your attitude while the lunar low is around. It's true that you could be slightly more pessimistic than would usually be the case but these are very temporary trends and should not be allowed to have a bearing on your long-term plans.

3 FRIDAY
Moon Age Day 7   Moon Sign Aries

There is a strongly competitive element about Libra at the moment and it is clear that you won't give in on anything once you have set your mind to it. Since there are some individuals around who are just as anxious to win as you are it looks as though the scene is set for some interesting and rewarding competitions.

4 SATURDAY
Moon Age Day 8   Moon Sign Taurus

Motivation is clearly the key to success at the moment, which is why you won't get a lot done if you keep taking on jobs you hate. Although unsavoury things have to be done these should be shared out fairly and there is no reason why you should always be at the front of the queue. Prompt someone else into taking a turn.

5 SUNDAY
Moon Age Day 9   Moon Sign Taurus

Try to widen your horizons and set out to make this a Sunday to remember. There are plenty of people around who would be more than willing to join in the fun. When Libra is on form you are the most charming and entertaining company around and you certainly can show yourself to be energetic under present planetary trends.

6 MONDAY
Moon Age Day 10   Moon Sign Gemini

Along comes a professional boost and this could turn out to be the most rewarding week of the month in the job stakes. Although you are active and enterprising, for the next couple of days you are also capable of being very contemplative. Your mindset represents a formidable combination, as the world is about to learn.

7 TUESDAY
Moon Age Day 11   Moon Sign Gemini

Career satisfaction can be achieved through being well organised and by getting others to work along lines you know to be sensible and productive. You possess good powers of persuasion and a very positive psychological approach that seems to be infectious. Not everyone is on your side now but most will be when it really matters.

8 WEDNESDAY
Moon Age Day 12   Moon Sign Cancer

This could prove to be a slightly testing day in a professional sense, though will be an easier time for those who are between jobs or retired. If your time is your own this would be a good day to try something completely new. Although you may be lacking very much money at present you remain, as always, resourceful.

9 THURSDAY
Moon Age Day 13   Moon Sign Cancer

You can now take a tough and uncompromising stance whenever necessary. This approach could shock someone who believed you to be a pushover but the surprising fact is that Libra can be one of the most stubborn of all the zodiac signs. At least some of your time now will be spent supporting someone who is having their own problems.

10 FRIDAY
Moon Age Day 14   Moon Sign Leo

This would be a great time to travel and although the weather still won't be up to much as far as Britain is concerned, there is a great big world out there that Libra loves to explore. However, if foreign shores are impossible at the moment find somewhere to go that at least feels like being in the sunshine.

11 SATURDAY
Moon Age Day 15   Moon Sign Leo

Be prepared to work very hard under present trends but the results will make all your efforts worthwhile. Nobody pitches in better than Libra and when you know you are on a winning streak you will put in far more effort than almost any other person. Now you push on simply because you wish to.

12 SUNDAY
Moon Age Day 16   Moon Sign Virgo

Be frugal with your purchases and, if possible, avoid spending too much money around now. It isn't that you are going to make yourself poor by doing so, simply that you are in line for some better bargains in a few days. In any case the things that are most important to you at the moment will cost you nothing at all.

13 MONDAY
Moon Age Day 17   Moon Sign Virgo

Friends should be both supportive and stimulating at this time and offer you the chance to relax a little, whilst they take some of the strain in potentially difficult situations. Life can be a breeze for those of you who are willing to take a back seat but at the moment Libra hates to let go of the reins and this can be a slight problem.

14 TUESDAY
Moon Age Day 18   Moon Sign Libra

The Moon now moves into your own sign of Libra, bringing the lunar high for February. It increases the level of your energy and also inclines you to be especially outgoing and gregarious. Lady Luck will be paying you a visit and you can afford to take a few more chances than has been the case so far this year.

15 WEDNESDAY *Moon Age Day 19   Moon Sign Libra*

It's time to imagine yourself doing new things and getting to know different people. Once you have played through the possibilities in your mind you can put them into action. This is the middle of a working week that can definitely be turned to your advantage and which should also bring material gains over the next few days.

16 THURSDAY *Moon Age Day 20   Moon Sign Libra*

You could find that at least some of what happens today is not in your best interests. Your associations with others may be somewhat strained and you have less patience than would normally be the case. Avoid situations that sound too good to be true because at the end of the day this is what they will turn out to be.

17 FRIDAY *Moon Age Day 21   Moon Sign Scorpio*

At work you may be demanding specific and very important changes. Whether everyone will fall in line with your plans remains to be seen but you are quite forceful at the moment and won't take no for an answer regarding issues you see as being important. For Libra at the moment that will be just about all of them.

18 SATURDAY *Moon Age Day 22   Moon Sign Scorpio*

Prospects look generally good for the weekend and you show a friendlier and calmer face to the outside world. Circumstances are pushing you along but you are more in control of the situation now and will be quite happy to allow others to take the lead in at least some matters. In sporting activities there is now everything to play for.

19 SUNDAY *Moon Age Day 23   Moon Sign Sagittarius*

This is a time to expand your horizons by increasing your general understanding. Gains come from fairly unexpected directions and you won't be ready for everything that comes your way. Reacting to situations quickly is not always your thing but you are quite responsive under present trends and life offers many gifts.

20 MONDAY   *Moon Age Day 24   Moon Sign Sagittarius*

Your career is very stimulating now and your social life is also likely to be on the up. Tasks that you take on are likely to be sorted in half the normal time and you should feel for the first time in a number of days that you are fully in command of yourself. Family members could prove demanding but you will take this in your stride.

21 TUESDAY   *Moon Age Day 25   Moon Sign Sagittarius*

This could be a good day to start an early spring clean. Although there is a very practical side to this, much of what takes place is within your own mind. It's time to dump things that are no longer of any use to you and replace them with interesting and stimulating new ventures. Thoughts of travel may well be on your mind.

22 WEDNESDAY   *Moon Age Day 26   Moon Sign Capricorn*

Social relationships should be providing some light relief and the pressures of the world at large tend to pass you by for a day or two. Socially speaking you will be on fine form and well suited to mixing with a variety of different people. Your charitable instincts are also well highlighted under present trends.

23 THURSDAY   *Moon Age Day 27   Moon Sign Capricorn*

An increase in the number of your responsibilities at work could leave you feeling solely in charge of everything and that colleagues don't want to know. However, there are gains to be made because people who count are noticing you. Don't take on more than you can reasonably handle but do jobs you have to undertake with your usual thoroughness.

24 FRIDAY   *Moon Age Day 28   Moon Sign Aquarius*

You should be making the most of friendship at this stage of the week and though you are not quite as responsive as would normally be the case, you are well liked and respected. It is often the case that others have a greater love of you than you do of yourself. Just listen to what people say and you will feel instantly happier.

25 SATURDAY *Moon Age Day 0   Moon Sign Aquarius*

Today ambitions and goals are not really central to your purpose. Strong social instincts surround you on all sides and what you really want to do right now is to be in the company of your friends. A shopping spree might be good but you won't find the sort of bargains that are likely to be on offer from Monday onwards.

26 SUNDAY *Moon Age Day 1   Moon Sign Aquarius*

Right now you will feel a definite urge to express your individuality and your competitive instincts are pronounced. It is hard luck for anyone who tries to get the better of you under present planetary trends. On a more personal level you will have a kind and caring side to your nature but this won't be obvious out there in the wider world.

27 MONDAY *Moon Age Day 2   Moon Sign Pisces*

The pace of your work should quicken even more and life can be quite frenetic at times. There will be little time to simply sit and take stock and you need to force short periods of reflection if you are not to exhaust yourself. You won't take too kindly to receiving instruction from others – especially those you don't really trust.

28 TUESDAY *Moon Age Day 3   Moon Sign Pisces*

Fulfilment is now found in a sense of personal freedom and in the chance to do what takes your fancy. Get the routines out of the way early in the day and then set out on some sort of journey – even if it is only a journey of the mind. There are some restrictions on the way so make the most of present trends.

March

2017

1 WEDNESDAY
Moon Age Day 4   Moon Sign Aries

If it suddenly seems as though you are carrying a heavy load in terms of responsibilities you need to be aware that the lunar low is around. How you feel about life and the way things really are can be too entirely different things. This is nothing but a short interlude and one through which you can take useful and much-needed rest.

2 THURSDAY
Moon Age Day 5   Moon Sign Aries

On the way up the ladder of success you could find other people or awkward situations blocking your way. Avoid over-reacting and instead take time to relax. Tomorrow will bring gradually better trends and put you back on course. For the moment you would gain from spending valuable moments in a lover's embrace.

3 FRIDAY
Moon Age Day 6   Moon Sign Taurus

The impact that others have on you is quite strong at this time and it is clear that you are making the most favourable impression imaginable. This is not to suggest that everyone takes to you and there will be people who are difficult to deal with. One area of life that can work really well for you at present is romance.

4 SATURDAY
Moon Age Day 7   Moon Sign Taurus

Whilst you are very fast-thinking yourself at the moment you could be forced into the company of people who are much slower on the uptake. This could prove to be rather frustrating and you are going to have to display that important Libran patience in order to deal with the situation. Friends prove themselves to be loyal.

5 SUNDAY   *Moon Age Day 8   Moon Sign Gemini*

A good day is in store and this also proves to be a day during which positive actions on your part can save you a great deal of time later. Stay away from anything tedious or boring and, if possible, get out into the good fresh air. The first stirrings of spring are around and Libra appreciates the fact with great joy.

6 MONDAY   *Moon Age Day 9   Moon Sign Gemini*

You should find yourself in an idealistic frame of mind at the start of this week and won't take no for an answer when it comes to achieving some of your most longed-for objectives for the sake of other people. Your generosity knows no bounds and you show yourself to be inspirational in your approach to those around you.

7 TUESDAY   *Moon Age Day 10   Moon Sign Cancer*

A few conflicts are possible today. These come about partly because of the attitude of colleagues or friends but also because you are in such a forceful frame of mind yourself. At certain times it can be like an irresistible force meeting and immovable object – and even lovely Libra can be stubborn on occasions.

8 WEDNESDAY   *Moon Age Day 11   Moon Sign Cancer*

There are new friendships on the way, or at least the possibility of them, and you are about as sociable now as you will be during March. Spring is showing itself more every day and that suits you well because all Air-signs such as yours love the spring. You should be generally cheerful and find ways to lift the spirits of friends.

9 THURSDAY   *Moon Age Day 12   Moon Sign Leo*

This is a great time for getting together with like-minded individuals and a day during which you will be leaving less favoured colleagues or acquaintances very much alone. There is a good chance that you will be making new friends at this time, probably as a result of initiatives that are coming into your life through a change of attitude.

10 FRIDAY *Moon Age Day 13* *Moon Sign Leo*

It will be impossible to please everyone today and it is rather unlikely that you will be trying to do so. Better by far to concentrate on one or two specific individuals – the sort of people who respond well to your personality for most of the time. Romance is looking good, especially for Librans who are now actively looking for love.

11 SATURDAY *Moon Age Day 14* *Moon Sign Virgo*

Your thoughts and moods fluctuate somewhat this weekend and you may discover that you are able to overcome past problems simply by looking at them in a new and revolutionary way. A break from the norm is called for in your social and personal life too. The more you surprise others – the greater your personal satisfaction will be.

12 SUNDAY *Moon Age Day 15* *Moon Sign Virgo*

It's time to keep up a busy schedule and to get stuck into practical matters. As this is the weekend you will also be planning social events and, perhaps, enjoyable outings. In almost every sense you are now looking ahead and will be able to see the future much more clearly than has been the case for a few weeks.

13 MONDAY *Moon Age Day 16* *Moon Sign Virgo*

You tend to be attracted to freedom-loving individuals today and that's good because such people can help you to broaden your own horizons. Attitude is very important when you are approaching anything new and if you believe in yourself there is very little that you cannot achieve. Every situation today is a learning experience.

14 TUESDAY *Moon Age Day 17* *Moon Sign Libra*

The lunar high returns and brings with it a sudden surge in energy and a great desire to get things done. New projects are in store and you can break down barriers from the past in order to get what you want from life. Bringing others round to your point of view should be child's play under present astrological trends.

15 WEDNESDAY   *Moon Age Day 18   Moon Sign Libra*

Get an early start today and pitch into important tasks. You are half way towards anything at all whilst the Moon occupies your zodiac sign and will show yourself to be willing to work long and hard to achieve your objectives. Somehow you will also find the time today to enjoy yourself and to entertain those around you.

16 THURSDAY   *Moon Age Day 19   Moon Sign Scorpio*

Think less about what you can take from either friendships or associations with colleagues and rather mull over what you can offer to them. It's a fact of life at the moment that the more you give, the greater will be your own satisfaction and success. New social encounters could turn into important friendships at this time.

17 FRIDAY   *Moon Age Day 20   Moon Sign Scorpio*

Success comes when you go with the flow more than has sometimes been the case across the last week or two. With changing astrological patterns, this becomes more likely. However there is just a chance that you will indulge in woolly thinking on occasions when a very decisive and direct attitude would be more helpful.

18 SATURDAY   *Moon Age Day 21   Moon Sign Scorpio*

You could find that others are more than willing to lighten your load now by lending a timely helping hand. Whether or not this will always be welcome remains to be seen because you are fairly self-possessed at the moment. All the same you will recognise the care that people are showing and will tend to respond in kind.

19 SUNDAY   *Moon Age Day 22   Moon Sign Sagittarius*

Your community spirit is generally strong and at the moment you will probably be lending a hand in a charitable sense or in some way that benefits your community. People are likely to approach you for advice and even if you feel you are less than qualified to oblige you will at least listen. That's the most important part.

20 MONDAY   *Moon Age Day 23   Moon Sign Sagittarius*

You remain very sociable and warm when dealing with people generally. This is Libra at its best and your charity-minded attitude will be much noticed. It would be best today to get tedious or boring jobs out of the way before you commit yourself to tasks you relish and which will take up much of your thinking power.

21 TUESDAY   *Moon Age Day 24   Moon Sign Capricorn*

If someone is trying to put the dampener on things the best thing you can do is to ignore them and to carry on in your own sweet way. You may be better off on your own today, at least when it comes to work. This is because colleagues are having their own problems – most of which are being created by negative attitudes.

22 WEDNESDAY   *Moon Age Day 25   Moon Sign Capricorn*

Consideration for the feelings of others might prevent you from taking significant steps towards a chosen objective. You can get round this potential problem by talking to individuals concerned and by explaining what you intend to do. It is unlikely that you would be refused any reasonable request under present trends.

23 THURSDAY   *Moon Age Day 26   Moon Sign Capricorn*

You may enjoy a great social and romantic lifestyle at this time. You could make new friends, or gain the approval of colleagues or bosses at work. What you don't need at the moment is someone telling you how every detail of your life should be arranged. If this happens, put the person responsible straight.

24 FRIDAY   *Moon Age Day 27   Moon Sign Aquarius*

Future prospects continue to look good and social developments especially will be on your mind. Potential disputes with loved ones may demand all your patience but if you refuse to get annoyed you will win out in the end. Someone you care about deeply may have something of great importance to divulge very soon.

25 SATURDAY   *Moon Age Day 28   Moon Sign Aquarius*

The sort of people you meet today will be thought-provoking and extremely interesting. It's a fact that you will be very committed to progress at the moment and will use any means at your disposal to get ahead. This could lead to you being more up-front than might sometimes be the case and there is no place for shyness.

26 SUNDAY   *Moon Age Day 29   Moon Sign Pisces*

Social discussions and important decisions are part of what today has to offer. You might not feel quite as confident to make up your mind as was clearly the case earlier in the month but with good support and sound common sense you should get on well enough. Keep abreast of current affairs and take an interest in your locality.

27 MONDAY   *Moon Age Day 0   Moon Sign Pisces*

There can be a slight downside to romance at the start of this particular week but any difficulties exist more in your mind than in reality. Remember to keep people informed of your present mindset because if you fail to do so you could run into difficulties created more or less entirely by the approaching lunar low.

28 TUESDAY   *Moon Age Day 1   Moon Sign Aries*

This is the time to slow down and to take a break. The lunar low makes it harder for you to be progressive, either in your attitude or in terms of practical moves. It would be better by far at the moment to watch and wait, whilst at the same time taking a few hours to yourself for quiet contemplation in the way that only Libra can.

29 WEDNESDAY   *Moon Age Day 2   Moon Sign Aries*

Your physical vitality is likely to be rather low but that doesn't mean you will be in any way unhappy. It's simply a case of going with the flow and treading water more than you usually would. Instead of trying to make everything work out the way you want, watch for a while. Some things will come good of their own accord.

30 THURSDAY   *Moon Age Day 3   Moon Sign Taurus*

Your capacity for sound judgement can be somewhat diminished, which is why it would certainly not be sensible to spend large amounts of money today unless you know extremely well what you are doing – and why. Pause for thought and take on board the advice of people who may know better than you do.

31 FRIDAY   *Moon Age Day 4   Moon Sign Taurus*

Your plans and ideas now begin to take on a practical form and any slight difficulties you have been encountering have done no more than to sharpen your intellect and your determination. Get on with projects you started earlier in the month and be willing to put in that extra bit of effort that you know can make all the difference.

April

2017

1 SATURDAY
Moon Age Day 5   Moon Sign Gemini

There isn't much doubt that you are outspoken today, even though there will be times when you really ought to bite your tongue. Such situations usually come about when Libra is defending someone else and that is likely to be the scenario now. Just make certain you know your facts before really having a go at anyone.

2 SUNDAY
Moon Age Day 6   Moon Sign Gemini

Around this time you should be taking a break from ordinary routines so that you can spend time thinking about your life as a whole and where it is presently leading you. A few minor alterations might be necessary and though these don't seem like much they can have a tremendous bearing on your longer-term future.

3 MONDAY
Moon Age Day 7   Moon Sign Cancer

It isn't so much what it is going on in front of your face that you find so appealing today but rather what is happening behind the scenes. It's clear that your curiosity is aroused and that you will not stop moving stones just to see what is under them. Just take care not to annoy anyone else by appearing to be nosey.

4 TUESDAY
Moon Age Day 8   Moon Sign Cancer

Relax and trust that most matters will turn out well in the long run. This is not a time to exhibit undue anxiety, if only because you will telegraph the fact to others and make them worry too. In any case most of what you are anxious about is either unimportant or will soon disappear like the morning mist.

5 WEDNESDAY   *Moon Age Day 9   Moon Sign Leo*

Apply a little self-discipline today and in your dealings with others it is important to sort out the wheat from the chaff. In a practical sense you should only throw in your lot with those who have proven themselves to be reliable and capable. Co-operation is very important now but so is careful selection before you commit yourself.

6 THURSDAY   *Moon Age Day 10   Moon Sign Leo*

It could be that you feel like getting away from routines today, though it's more likely you will be planning a break for the weekend. For now you remain generally busy but it will be very easy to grow bored with routines and to tinker with things as a result. This can be quite entertaining but could lead to a few problems.

7 FRIDAY   *Moon Age Day 11   Moon Sign Leo*

When it comes to personal attachments you may not be going through the best period you are likely to experience either this month or even this year. Present planetary trends can sometimes make attachments look less than sparkling. Much depends on your own attitude and the effort you put in personally.

8 SATURDAY   *Moon Age Day 12   Moon Sign Virgo*

Mental talents and the ability to communicate your ideas and opinions to others are definitely strong at the moment. This could be a crackerjack of a weekend and particularly so in a social sense. Avoid getting tied down too much with domestic responsibility and do your best to mix as much as possible.

9 SUNDAY   *Moon Age Day 13   Moon Sign Virgo*

It might be necessary to strike a balance between work and home around now, so if you have some time to yourself on this Sunday, take a few moments to be on your own and to think. There will be distractions about but these will not prevent you from finding a little corner where you can meditate in peace.

10 MONDAY ☿ *Moon Age Day 14   Moon Sign Libra*

Self-confidence and a simple faith in your own ability is all you need to make a success of today. With the lunar high on your side it is very likely that some good fortune will be paying a visit to your life, though it has to be said that in the main you make your own luck at present. Above all, you are very idealistic.

11 TUESDAY ☿ *Moon Age Day 15   Moon Sign Libra*

This is a time when you should be looking at far-reaching plans and working out how to make them work much earlier than you might previously have expected. You remain optimistic, know what you want from life and can easily get the people on board who will be in the best possible position to help you out.

12 WEDNESDAY ☿ *Moon Age Day 16   Moon Sign Scorpio*

Personal relationships won't be doing you too many favours today, which is why if you are wise you will stick to friendships and keep your view of things light and superficial. By tomorrow you will be once again committed to looking at romance or deep commitments but that is simply not the way you are made at the moment.

13 THURSDAY ☿ *Moon Age Day 17   Moon Sign Scorpio*

It may not be important to you today to seek personal recognition of your achievements. What matters more is making certain that things are done efficiently and properly. It will be easy to become annoyed with those who won't do what you tell them or people who seem determined to throw a spanner in the works simply to be mischievous.

14 FRIDAY ☿ *Moon Age Day 18   Moon Sign Scorpio*

As Friday dawns trends favour communications and you will be talking freely to just about anyone you come across. You will be happy to go on a shopping spree, or even to have a trip out with your partner or a friend. What wouldn't be good today would be to stick around usual places, doing the same old things.

15 SATURDAY ☿ *Moon Age Day 19* *Moon Sign Sagittarius*

This should be a promising weekend and one during which you can reach out into new areas and try things you haven't thought about before. Travelling is especially well highlighted under present trends and you may be moving about for work or leisure and pleasure. You have great energy and solid ideas.

16 SUNDAY ☿ *Moon Age Day 20* *Moon Sign Sagittarius*

Enjoy the companionship of friends and give your best when involved in group activities outside of work. If you are a sporting Libran this weekend should bring its own successes but you might not yet quite have the winning punch that will be more obvious later in April. If you need more money – look around.

17 MONDAY ☿ *Moon Age Day 21* *Moon Sign Capricorn*

Your professional life is likely to mean a lot to you today and you will be concentrating very hard in order to get things right. Others will be offering timely assistance but more so if you are willing to ask for it. Sometimes Libra can be too proud for its own good. Call in a few favours – you won't be refused.

18 TUESDAY ☿ *Moon Age Day 22* *Moon Sign Capricorn*

It could be difficult to adopt a leading role in practical and work-based situations under present but very temporary planetary trends. The chances are that you lack a little confidence and that you won't have the level of certainty you need to be willing to push yourself forward too much. Things alter in a day or two.

19 WEDNESDAY ☿ *Moon Age Day 23* *Moon Sign Capricorn*

Partnerships should seem to improve as the planetary picture begins to line up in your favour. Any past uncertainty should be out of the window and there is room for optimism, even regarding issues that have caused you some stress in the past. Most of the really important people will seem to be on your side at this time.

20 THURSDAY ☿ *Moon Age Day 24   Moon Sign Aquarius*

You can afford to allow a little excitement to rise to the surface and you must avoid thinking that something is about to go wrong. In friendships you are steadfast and supportive, which could prove to be very important to someone who has been going through a rather hard time over the last few weeks or months.

21 FRIDAY ☿ *Moon Age Day 25   Moon Sign Aquarius*

If you want to feel secure and settled, as most Librans do, you can do a great deal right now to improve on personal securities. If life hasn't been too easy of late you can be fairly certain that at least some situations will be taking a turn for the better. Trust your own abilities and also put some faith in your loved ones.

22 SATURDAY ☿ *Moon Age Day 26   Moon Sign Pisces*

You like to go to places that are fun and which offer some sort of personal reward. That is exactly what you are likely to be doing at the moment. Take the lead and allow others to follow you if they wish. Slowly but surely you are beginning to demonstrate that Libra is quite capable of being at the front and offering sound instructions.

23 SUNDAY ☿ *Moon Age Day 27   Moon Sign Pisces*

Your organisational powers are now at their best, especially so when applied to practical matters. You may not be the best at the theory of matters for the moment, but when it comes to getting your sleeves rolled up you are second to none. Avoid becoming involved in arguments of any sort, especially if they are in the family.

24 MONDAY ☿ *Moon Age Day 28   Moon Sign Pisces*

You have a natural ability to communicate and should be getting on well with most of the people who play a part in your life this week. If you are working you can expect to make some sort of progress but those Librans who are at home may be the luckiest of all. Take hold of your partner's hand and lead them somewhere magical.

25 TUESDAY ☿ *Moon Age Day 0   Moon Sign Aries*

The Moon now moves into Aries, bringing the lunar low for you and one of the quieter interludes of the month. There isn't really much point in knocking your head against a wall because you won't get everything you want today. It would be better by far to watch and wait, whilst you plan in detail for what lies ahead of you.

26 WEDNESDAY ☿ *Moon Age Day 1   Moon Sign Aries*

Many issues could be resolved at this time – if you could only summon up the energy to think about them. Things are the way they are for the moment and you will only become frustrated if you try to alter anything significant right now. By tomorrow you are much more dynamic but for the moment you should relax and float.

27 THURSDAY ☿ *Moon Age Day 2   Moon Sign Taurus*

A time for new approaches and different ideas has dawned. Make use of all these positive planetary trends and give yourself over to new incentives. Listen carefully to suggestions that are being made at this time and co-operate with business partners. Things also look particularly good as far as your personal life is concerned.

28 FRIDAY ☿ *Moon Age Day 3   Moon Sign Taurus*

This is a day for self-discipline and for being slightly more thoughtful before you commit yourself to anything that looks in the least difficult. You can avoid pitfalls by simply thinking things through but there is a slight tendency for your enthusiasm to get ahead of your common sense for a day or two.

29 SATURDAY ☿ *Moon Age Day 4   Moon Sign Gemini*

Your present circumstances can be a little confused but you still have a great sense of purpose. As today wears on slightly negative trends have less of a bearing on your life and more positive associations take over. By the evening you should be in the pink and feeling extremely confident about your life.

30 SUNDAY ☿ *Moon Age Day 5   Moon Sign Gemini*

Don't ignore your intuition, which tends to be extremely strong at the moment. That little voice inside your head that tells you to proceed or to stay where you are will be your best guide today and can be useful in almost any situation. There are potential gains to be made for Librans who work at the weekend.

♎ May

2017

1 MONDAY ☿ *Moon Age Day 6   Moon Sign Cancer*

Happiness and satisfaction are likely to come along predominantly as a result of social engagements and attachments. You enjoy being in the spotlight and won't mind at all when you realise that others have been talking about you. Fortunately most of what they have to say is very complimentary and you can bask in their praise.

2 TUESDAY ☿ *Moon Age Day 7   Moon Sign Cancer*

You need to encourage better family support all round, and not just for your own sake. Convincing others to pull together is part of what today is about and you have what it takes to get others to follow your lead. Libra can be quite contemplative under present trends but that won't prevent you from speaking your mind too.

3 WEDNESDAY ☿ *Moon Age Day 8   Moon Sign Leo*

Besides being creative and very affectionate at the moment you show yourself to be deeply magnetic and very attractive to most of the people you meet today. You have a slight tendency to be bossy but this may be no bad thing if it means you can persuade someone to do something that they have been avoiding strenuously.

4 THURSDAY *Moon Age Day 9   Moon Sign Leo*

Domestic and family issues could be taking up a fair percentage of your time and you show immense consideration for the well-being and general feelings of those around you. Fairly untypically you can be quite intransigent if you feel yourself pushed into a corner but in the main you are more relaxed than would often seem to be the case.

5 FRIDAY   *Moon Age Day 10   Moon Sign Virgo*

Take some time out to organise things, not only in a material sense but also with regard to the way your mind is working at present. If you don't, you could be accused of being muddled in your thoughts and competitors can use this against you. A few hours out of the social maelstrom will probably appeal to you a great deal today.

6 SATURDAY   *Moon Age Day 11   Moon Sign Virgo*

There are different views around at the moment and this period can be quite informative. Libra is always anxious to learn and that is particularly the case at the moment. Life itself is your schoolroom and you never tire of realising that there is something else to be taken on board. Today should be very entertaining.

7 SUNDAY   *Moon Age Day 12   Moon Sign Libra*

It's time for you to press ahead with big plans and to make yourself the master of your own destiny to a much greater extent. You won't have any difficulty getting on with anyone you meet and that's important whilst the lunar high is around. There are so many gains to be made and all of them are about people in one way or another.

8 MONDAY   *Moon Age Day 13   Moon Sign Libra*

Short-term goals are dealt with at lightning speed and longer-term ambitions won't take too much longer. Whilst others are thinking about acting, you have things sorted. This can be a great advantage because it means that you are pushing ahead much quicker than either you or almost anyone else thought possible.

9 TUESDAY   *Moon Age Day 14   Moon Sign Libra*

There are certain matters rising to the surface today and you probably won't care for the look of all of them. You could get slightly crabby and over-concerned with details that are not of the slightest importance in the greater scheme of things. It would be better to be alone on occasion today, rather than to fly off the handle.

10 WEDNESDAY   *Moon Age Day 15   Moon Sign Scorpio*

Your judgement is sound in professional matters and you have what it takes to put yourself in the best possible position at work. Librans who have been thinking about a change of career may be well advised to look around at the moment as there is a reasonable chance that a new opportunity will fall into your lap.

11 THURSDAY   *Moon Age Day 16   Moon Sign Scorpio*

It is impossible for you to be in two places at once, so if you co-operate successfully with others you may be able to delegate some tasks that you can't handle to them. Do what you can to show yourself to be capable and don't hedge your bets when it comes to decisions. It's time to show your mettle.

12 FRIDAY   *Moon Age Day 17   Moon Sign Sagittarius*

You can expect to get your own way a great deal with practical matters and could be quite acquisitive under present trends. Fight the urge to splurge money on things you don't really need. The result of doing so under present planetary trends is almost certain to be a large amount of buyer's remorse.

13 SATURDAY   *Moon Age Day 18   Moon Sign Sagittarius*

Avoid tensions at home by speaking your mind, though as diplomatically as you can manage. If you are feeling slightly under the weather you would probably respond well to a breath of fresh air because Libra is, of necessity, a lover of the outdoors. This will be especially true if you have been cooped up for some days.

14 SUNDAY   *Moon Age Day 19   Moon Sign Sagittarius*

Recognition of your own ego is not only important at the moment – it's vital. You will enjoy entertaining others and as far as your home is concerned it's likely to be a case of open house. Libra is now acting on impulse to a much greater extent than would normally be the case. Use your present influence at every opportunity.

15 MONDAY   *Moon Age Day 20   Moon Sign Capricorn*

New financial beginnings now become entirely possible and with tremendous intuition working on your behalf you are hardly likely to make mistakes when it comes to cash. As always you are careful and astute in your dealings and will also find time today to show tremendous support for a friend or your partner.

16 TUESDAY   *Moon Age Day 21   Moon Sign Capricorn*

Confusion is possible in relationships and some extra effort will need to be made if you are to fully understand what other people are talking about. Sit down with them and have a long chat. On the way you might learn something important about yourself, as well as establishing new ground rules that are going to suit everyone in the future.

17 WEDNESDAY   *Moon Age Day 22   Moon Sign Aquarius*

Don't rush when it comes to making judgements about others. The fact is that you could so easily be wrong and as a result could say or do something that is totally inappropriate. In a practical sense you are active and enterprising, but you won't get exactly what you want without making some important compromises on the way.

18 THURSDAY   *Moon Age Day 23   Moon Sign Aquarius*

This should be a good day for expressing yourself and for getting on side with people who seem to have had some problems with your recent behaviour or attitudes. It's time to heal a wound from the past as well, at the same time putting issues behind you that are no longer relevant. Start a new health regime at any time now.

19 FRIDAY   *Moon Age Day 24   Moon Sign Pisces*

Beware of coming on too strong, especially in terms of personal attachments. You can achieve far more by being just slightly cool and a tad aloof. If you retain a certain air of mystery you become more intriguing and someone special will search all the more to find out what makes you tick. Hang on to cash for the moment.

20 SATURDAY   *Moon Age Day 25   Moon Sign Pisces*

In terms of your love life it is possible that you will find your feelings running slightly contrary to what you might have expected. There is a search for personal freedom going on and you may resent the fact that someone else appears to be taking over a part of your life you see as private. The chances are, though, that you are over-reacting big style.

21 SUNDAY   *Moon Age Day 26   Moon Sign Pisces*

Look out for a positive time for new beginnings. Anything that has been sitting around in your life and not offering you anything could well be abandoned under present trends and life has a knowing knack of offering newer and better opportunities at every turn. That's why it is worth keeping your eyes open in the coming week.

22 MONDAY   *Moon Age Day 27   Moon Sign Aries*

Your spirits are inclined to flag just a little today, at the onset of the lunar low. Avoid reacting to this and do your best to show yourself as being confident and not in the least disturbed by the odd setback. With the Sun in its present position you can probably ignore a few peculiar situations too and carry on more or less as normal.

23 TUESDAY   *Moon Age Day 28   Moon Sign Aries*

You may simply have to make the best of things today and get what you can from life, despite the fact that some elements of it seem to be working against you. This isn't really the case but you are hardly at your most optimistic during the lunar low. Let others makes some of the decisions today and be prepared to delegate.

24 WEDNESDAY   *Moon Age Day 29   Moon Sign Taurus*

In a professional sense older or wiser people could help you on your way, even if you can't actually make any progress today. You are looking ahead, planning your strategy and laying down guidelines for later. At the same time this is a day that positively demands the sort of social mixing you generally love.

25 THURSDAY
Moon Age Day 0   Moon Sign Taurus

There are changes to your financial situation – some of which could be fairly surprising and quite immediate. Not that you need to worry about any of this because you are well protected in a planetary sense. Almost everything that is going on in your life at this time will work to your eventual interest – just wait a while and see.

26 FRIDAY
Moon Age Day 1   Moon Sign Gemini

Getting something right first time could be fairly important, if only because you are so busy and there isn't very much time to spare. You are able to pursue most objectives with great zeal and there are potential gains around most corners. This should be especially true at work but your social life could also be quite productive right now.

27 SATURDAY
Moon Age Day 2   Moon Sign Gemini

You will benefit from being surrounded by a good cross-section of people today. With the planets in their present position, it isn't any one sort of individual that interests you but humanity as a whole. You will be more gregarious than usual, less shy when you are with strangers and definitely inclined to speak your opinions to everyone.

28 SUNDAY
Moon Age Day 3   Moon Sign Cancer

Working hard to get what you want is never a problem for you and you can certainly put in the hours and the effort at this time. Meanwhile, if there is something you have wanted for a while but haven't been able to find, why not take yourself off on a search now? A car boot sale or similar could reveal odd, unusual or quirky items that fascinate you now.

29 MONDAY
Moon Age Day 4   Moon Sign Cancer

Imagine the joy of having things working out exactly as you had hoped and planned? Well imagine no longer because if you put in just a little more effort, that is what will happen. Be confident and stay fixed on your goals. It might not be possible to get everything you want today but there are signs that you are well on the way.

30 TUESDAY   *Moon Age Day 5   Moon Sign Leo*

Don't get carried away with impractical ideas and make sure that you are in the know when it comes to situations related to your work. Something from your past may need looking at again, and this time in a new light. At home it's a case of 'off with the old and one with the new'. You won't tolerate mess or untidiness at this time.

31 WEDNESDAY   *Moon Age Day 6   Moon Sign Leo*

You can make important changes to yourself and your life today. Stand aside from everyday concerns and treat the day as something special for you. Stop absorbing so many responsibilities and make up your mind to be more casual in your approach. You will be amazed how much difference this will make to your life.

June 2017

1 THURSDAY
Moon Age Day 7   Moon Sign Virgo

You could be asked to involve yourself in moneymaking ventures and although these might look quite exciting you would be well advised to think carefully before embarking. Money is the only area of your life that needs special attention under present trends and you certainly should not part with cash willy-nilly.

2 FRIDAY
Moon Age Day 8   Moon Sign Virgo

A boost to your ego is on the way, maybe as a result of the things others are saying to you but wherever it comes from you should be feeling quite pleased with yourself before the day is out. You can certainly cut a dash in social situations and, as usual, you manage to be elegant often without much effort.

3 SATURDAY
Moon Age Day 9   Moon Sign Virgo

Avoid making any rash, impulse purchases for the moment. Venus is making you rather inclined to splash out too freely, maybe on things you don't need or which you could get cheaper elsewhere. The luxury-loving side of your nature is the culprit and this is a part of you that sometimes has to be kept under control.

4 SUNDAY
Moon Age Day 10   Moon Sign Libra

You are almost certain to feel far more dynamic than usual and for that you can thank the present position of the Moon. Anything you have shied away from in the past because you lacked confidence can now be approached with impunity. Don't take no for an answer and stick to your guns when you know your reasoning is sound.

5 MONDAY · · · · · · · · · · · · · · · · · · *Moon Age Day 11 · · · Moon Sign Libra*

Look out for a few minor triumphs and don't be surprised if you discover that you are practically everyone's cup of tea at the moment. Now is the right time to push for something you really want and the only possible difficulty comes if you continue to spend money you probably don't have on things you really don't need.

6 TUESDAY · · · · · · · · · · · · · · · · *Moon Age Day 12 · · · Moon Sign Scorpio*

Your partner or a close family member could well be coming up with some ideas that, although well intentioned, are either impractical or downright impossible. It's up to you to put them back on course, though this might not be very easy. A mixture of diplomacy and firmness is probably the best way forward.

7 WEDNESDAY · · · · · · · · · · · · *Moon Age Day 13 · · · Moon Sign Scorpio*

Most of your effort today is likely to be focused on practical matters and efforts you are making to get on better in a material sense. Relationships figure less in your thinking than might usually be the case but this is only because you have your hands full in other ways and don't have too much time for personal commitment.

8 THURSDAY · · · · · · · · · · · · · *Moon Age Day 14 · · · Moon Sign Sagittarius*

This ought to be a fairly satisfying day and is a time during which money matters are easier to address than might have seemed to be the case in the recent past. Quick successes are more likely and you are now inclined to speak your mind and to ignore the possible consequences. People will marvel at your present wit.

9 FRIDAY · · · · · · · · · · · · · · · · · · · *Moon Age Day 15 · · · Moon Sign Sagittarius*

This could be a good day to talk to someone special and to make new attachments from what were previously only acquaintances. Someone thinks you are wonderful and will be quite likely to tell you so under present planetary trends. How you react to all the compliments remains to be seen. Try to do more than simply blushing.

10 SATURDAY   *Moon Age Day 16   Moon Sign Sagittarius*

You may prefer to stay at home and to allow others to visit you this weekend. All the same you are not isolating yourself and will mix freely with family members, friends and neighbours. In amongst the mix you need as much familiarity and personal support as you can get – if only because you feel slightly insecure.

11 SUNDAY   *Moon Age Day 17   Moon Sign Capricorn*

Although things are likely to be working out well as far as the wider world is concerned, there are still likely to be a few minor problems to deal with at home. Set aside some time to address these and don't avoid issues simply because you don't like the look of them. A few wise words right now can work wonders.

12 MONDAY   *Moon Age Day 18   Moon Sign Capricorn*

Independence is gradually becoming your middle name. You certainly won't take kindly to being told what to do and even relaxed Libra can be quite stubborn when necessary. The fact is that you think you know best for most of the time at the moment and you will be very anxious to follow your own notions to their ultimate conclusions.

13 TUESDAY   *Moon Age Day 19   Moon Sign Aquarius*

Enterprising ideas come thick and fast and it's all you can do to keep up with your own thought processes. Don't be too quick to jump to conclusions and try to follow through once you have started a particular course of action. All in all this might turn out to be one of the most progressive days for quite some time.

14 WEDNESDAY   *Moon Age Day 20   Moon Sign Aquarius*

Self-expression is now the key to happiness so it is worth searching for just the right words to tell others how you feel. You won't be at all keen to get involved in anything dirty or unsavoury and would be quite willing at the moment to let others do some of the less pleasant jobs. The only problem is that they might complain about it.

15 THURSDAY   *Moon Age Day 21   Moon Sign Aquarius*

A certain family issue could arise at this time that will come to take on an importance far beyond what seems either necessary or prudent. Once you have dealt with this issue you will be free to pursue your own course but even then there are likely to be frequent little issues cropping up that demand your time and cause frustration.

16 FRIDAY   *Moon Age Day 22   Moon Sign Pisces*

You have a real talent for financial matters at the moment. Such matters are likely to be uppermost in your at this time and there are ways and means to make yourself better off. Look at all potential deals carefully and bring your special common sense to bear upon issues that have a bearing on your home life.

17 SATURDAY   *Moon Age Day 23   Moon Sign Pisces*

What you need will generally be at hand, even if you don't always realise it immediately. You may find yourself undoing something that wasn't done right in the first place and that could mean upsetting someone. You are quite capable of being diplomatic but there are times when it won't be easy to bite your tongue.

18 SUNDAY   *Moon Age Day 24   Moon Sign Aries*

A planetary lull comes your way and although there isn't much you can do about it, you can nullify the worst of the lunar low by simply slowing down a little. It doesn't matter how much you try to get on today, there is something holding you back. Realising this and relaxing is nine tenths of the battle.

19 MONDAY   *Moon Age Day 25   Moon Sign Aries*

Some Librans could simply feel exhausted today but at least if you do you can be reassured that this is a very temporary situation. You have been working very hard in one way or another and there is nothing to say you should keep pushing, especially just for today. Do something different and you will feel on top of the world.

20 TUESDAY   *Moon Age Day 26   Moon Sign Taurus*

Expect a busy time at work as your organisational skills are put to the test. It is vital that you don't miss too much of whatever is going on out there in the big wide world and you will be very keen to be involved in new efforts that are being planned close to your home. You can do two things at once but ten might be a rather tall order!

21 WEDNESDAY   *Moon Age Day 27   Moon Sign Taurus*

Financial goals reach concrete conclusions for many and there are new gains to think about that have a bearing on your social life. There is a positive emphasis right now on your personal economic circumstances both at home and with regard to efforts outside of the home. You show strong charitable inclinations at this time.

22 THURSDAY   *Moon Age Day 28   Moon Sign Gemini*

Now you can be at your most gregarious and it is clear that you will be fun to have around. It should be possible to turn all this good-natured banter in the direction of practical matters – which now tend to get done in a fraction of the normal time. Limit what you actually take on otherwise you could be chasing your tail all day.

23 FRIDAY   *Moon Age Day 29   Moon Sign Gemini*

You could find that you are somewhat too sensitive for your own good at times today and this is probably because you don't have quite the level of confidence in yourself that has been the case recently. Casual remarks made by others should not be taken out of context and it might be sensible to adopt a guarded approach to others.

24 SATURDAY   *Moon Age Day 0   Moon Sign Cancer*

You will enjoy a harmonious attitude at home and won't want to get involved in deep discussions or rows with anyone. If you find it difficult to avoid these you need to remove yourself from the field of conflict. It is likely that you will also be enjoying the changing seasons now that the summer is beginning to show itself.

25 SUNDAY
Moon Age Day 1   Moon Sign Cancer

The time has come to be slightly more self-centred than would usually be the case for a Libran. However, once you have your own house in order you will be in a better position to help others along too. In the initial stages of any plan you may have to decide things for yourself, though if possible without upsetting others.

26 MONDAY
Moon Age Day 2   Moon Sign Leo

Communications represent the best area of life and you are also likely to be very committed to group activities, both at work and in a social sense. Look out for good news that is likely to be coming your way at any time now and make the most of even little opportunities to get more money flowing into your bank account.

27 TUESDAY
Moon Age Day 3   Moon Sign Leo

There could be a degree of nostalgia to deal with, whilst in a social sense both family members and friends unite to show you a high degree of support. Family matters could prove to be amongst your greatest pleasures at this stage of the week and the impending start of a new month will find you madly planning ways to please your partner.

28 WEDNESDAY
Moon Age Day 4   Moon Sign Leo

Now it would be especially useful and rewarding to throw in your lot with others. Group activities are the mainstay of this midweek period and you are less likely than is occasionally the case to go it alone. The more compliments that flood in, the happier you are likely to feel about yourself and the path you take through life.

29 THURSDAY
Moon Age Day 5   Moon Sign Virgo

Opportunities stand around you on every side and you are now in a time of potential good fortune. With greater luck attending most of your efforts you should be quite willing to go that extra mile in order to achieve important objectives. There is help at hand if you need it but the chances are that you will want to lead the field when possible.

30 FRIDAY
Moon Age Day 6   Moon Sign Virgo

A conflict may arise between domestic and social demands. It's clear that you are burning the candle at both ends right now and perhaps this is a situation that needs dealing with before you fall over altogether. All the same Libra is a fairly resilient zodiac sign and you can keep going long after many people have gone to bed.

July

2017

1 SATURDAY
Moon Age Day 7   Moon Sign Libra

Your intuitive and mental powers receive a fresh boost of stimulation as the Moon returns to your zodiac sign. The lunar high this time coincides with the weekend so much of your energy is likely to be given to social and family pursuits. This would be the best time of the year to think about taking a holiday.

2 SUNDAY
Moon Age Day 8   Moon Sign Libra

Opportunity is certainly knocking on your door repeatedly around this time but there are so many possibilities about it will be difficult to follow up every potential gain. In any case you are not materially minded at the moment and the lunar high is more likely to stimulate your desire for fun in the company of those you love.

3 MONDAY
Moon Age Day 9   Moon Sign Scorpio

There ought to be a certain amount of ongoing success where money matters are concerned and you seem to have what it takes to be in the right place for a bargain or two this week. Your attitude is good and people are certainly keeping an eye on you. That means that working Librans could be in for advancement of some sort.

4 TUESDAY
Moon Age Day 10   Moon Sign Scorpio

Though your personal magnetism remains high you should take care not to be over confident and to blow one or two of your best plans simply because you aren't careful enough. Your approach with family members and even friends can be rather too positive and it might be best to tone your attitude down a little.

5 WEDNESDAY   *Moon Age Day 11   Moon Sign Scorpio*

A good dose of positive thinking can now have a tremendous bearing on your life and the general circumstances that surround you. Because you are so go-getting you won't let a single opportunity pass you by. It isn't that anything particularly special is happening – more that you handle what is around much more successfully.

6 THURSDAY   *Moon Age Day 12   Moon Sign Sagittarius*

In amongst the very busy pattern your life is taking you will find moments to enjoy family life and all that it offers. Today could be such a period and is a time when your ruling planet Venus has much to offer you. With loved ones you can be quieter and spend as much time listening as you do talking.

7 FRIDAY   *Moon Age Day 13   Moon Sign Sagittarius*

In terms of communication you are now in for a very hectic phase and this applies as much to your social life as it may to your work. Someone you haven't met for quite some time is likely to come back into your life and brings with them the chance of a replay of situations from the past. Keep one eye on the future, though.

8 SATURDAY   *Moon Age Day 14   Moon Sign Capricorn*

Positive thinking really can make it so – at least it can if you also put in that extra bit of effort that makes all the difference. There may be a chance that you will meet someone now who can be of real importance to you and that what they have to tell you will lead to a sea-change in attitude on your behalf.

9 SUNDAY   *Moon Age Day 15   Moon Sign Capricorn*

A marvellous mental boost is on the way when it comes to conversation and intellectual exchanges of any sort. You are as refined as Libra often is and will relish pleasant, sophisticated surroundings. It is also possible that you will be thinking about making changes to your home at any time during this period.

10 MONDAY *Moon Age Day 16   Moon Sign Capricorn*

You communicate well with friends but tend to stay away from individuals you find either contentious or troublesome to your spirit. With everything to play for in a material sense you will probably still opt for quiet and contemplation. You know instinctively that this is not exactly the right day during which to act.

11 TUESDAY *Moon Age Day 17   Moon Sign Aquarius*

Right now communication matters are set to make life both interesting and varied. The accent is still on those you know and love and less on your association with the world at large. Nevertheless, what you hear and see outside of your home today is vital in terms of organising your future.

12 WEDNESDAY *Moon Age Day 18   Moon Sign Aquarius*

You are very warm and supportive to those people who are closest to you, but you are also good when dealing with acquaintances or strangers. Everyone has the right to see the best side of your nature at the moment and you could be going to tremendous lengths in order to satisfy the needs of a world for which you care deeply.

13 THURSDAY *Moon Age Day 19   Moon Sign Pisces*

Home and family are the issues that count the most with Libra at the moment and you continue to work hard on behalf of those you love. Elements of the past are still likely to replay in your mind and you are filled with positive emotions when it comes to expressing your affection. This is a warm and happy time.

14 FRIDAY *Moon Age Day 20   Moon Sign Pisces*

Colleagues or friends can bring out the best in you at the moment and you relish the attention of people you find interesting and stimulating. It's all about your mind around this time and your intellectual capacities seem somehow increased. The more high-flying the company – the better you will enjoy the experience.

15 SATURDAY
Moon Age Day 21   Moon Sign Aries

This is hardly going to be one of the best days of the month for you when it comes to capitalising on opportunities. It might be better not to try and to simply drift with the tide for a while. There is no harm in taking a short holiday from life and by tomorrow you should be getting back on course, and feeling less stressed.

16 SUNDAY
Moon Age Day 22   Moon Sign Aries

This may not be the most outgoing or exciting weekend you have ever known but it does have its good points. For one thing you are more willing to rest and relax, which considering the pace of your life recently has to be a good thing. At the same time you will have more time to listen to your partner or family members.

17 MONDAY
Moon Age Day 23   Moon Sign Aries

Domestic matters look as though they are likely to be the most rewarding area of life today, though that doesn't mean that you should diminish your efforts to get in on the commercial world too. In many respects this is almost certainly going to be a fairly routine sort of day, though nonetheless useful for that.

18 TUESDAY
Moon Age Day 24   Moon Sign Taurus

Strong views are likely to be aired today and you are not likely to accept comments with which you don't agree. Nevertheless there are occasions when it would be extremely sensible to count to ten. Losing your temper won't help and in any case it would spoil the wonderful reputation you are building up right now.

19 WEDNESDAY
Moon Age Day 25   Moon Sign Taurus

Keep your eyes and ears open for news and views, some of which is both surprising and interesting. Today should bring a great deal of variety, plus a desire for fresh fields and pastures new. This is not especially unusual at this time of year and can be catered for by planning or actually taking a holiday.

20 THURSDAY   *Moon Age Day 26   Moon Sign Gemini*

Certain career matters are now bearing fruit. If you have been looking for a new job, or merely a greater degree of responsibility with regard to your present career, now is the time to keep your eyes open. In some areas of life you appear to be on automatic pilot, though this won't be the case in terms of your personal relationships.

21 FRIDAY   *Moon Age Day 27   Moon Sign Gemini*

Now you are in a position to make a bigger impression on others. With your energy levels fully restored, and in possession of a great deal of charm, the time has come to ask for what you want. If you feel you are being unfairly treated in some way, today is a fine time to make your feelings known.

22 SATURDAY   *Moon Age Day 28   Moon Sign Cancer*

Certain discussions in the wider world could have an argumentative side to them, something you will probably want to avoid. Although you wish to put your point of view across, there isn't much point in making enemies on the way. A gentler approach works better, so defuse situations when you can.

23 SUNDAY   *Moon Age Day 0   Moon Sign Cancer*

Financial trends ought to be good, leading you to a sense of satisfaction in your life that might have been missing somewhat of late. There are opportunities to speak your mind in a romantic sense and so some excitement is on the cards. You need to find interesting things to do today, in the company of happy people.

24 MONDAY   *Moon Age Day 1   Moon Sign Leo*

Now you are forced back on your own wits, never a particularly bad state of affairs. All the practical skills at your disposal will be necessary in the days ahead, though you have a good potential map of the future in your head and a certainty about the way you want life to go. Stay determined.

25 TUESDAY *Moon Age Day 2   Moon Sign Leo*

Prepare yourself for a day of contrasts. Family issues should still be going well but you might not be able to get all your own way as far as personal matters are concerned. Meanwhile, the pressures that are being put on you at work could begin to show, with the result that you tell people exactly how you feel.

26 WEDNESDAY *Moon Age Day 3   Moon Sign Virgo*

A discussion with someone very close to you can lead to decisions that could not have been taken even a few days ago. There is a strong need for you to feel secure today and that can be catered for by simply talking to the people you love and live with. Reassurance can also come from the direction of friends.

27 THURSDAY *Moon Age Day 4   Moon Sign Virgo*

There are many things you want to get done today, but whether you get around to tackling them remains to be seen. What would really suit you best might be a change of scene and the chance to look at rolling oceans or high hills. If you are able to be in the company of people you really love, then so much the better.

28 FRIDAY *Moon Age Day 5   Moon Sign Libra*

This is probably the best part of the month for actually getting things done. The lunar high brings greater confidence and allows you to influence others in ways that may not have been possible earlier. This is especially true today with regard to family members, friends and, of course, your partner.

29 SATURDAY *Moon Age Day 6   Moon Sign Libra*

As was the case yesterday you can get your own way and make life work out more or less the way you would wish. Give yourself a pat on the back for something you have just achieved, but don't allow the situation to go to your head. There is plenty more to do, and right now you have the energy to move mountains.

30 SUNDAY
Moon Age Day 7   Moon Sign Libra

Trips down memory lane are fine but they don't butter any bread. It is in the world of practicalities that you tend to find yourself today and there are many issues that have to be addressed. Although you remain fairly busy, there should also be more than enough time to find ways in which you can have fun.

31 MONDAY
Moon Age Day 8   Moon Sign Scorpio

A few sharp comments made by you today might not go down very well with certain other people. You need to be very careful what you say around sensitive people, and you yourself can also be quite prickly. Stay around people you know well because they are less likely to react and you know what to expect.

August

2017

1 TUESDAY
Moon Age Day 9   Moon Sign Scorpio

Matters of the heart have a lot going for them at the moment and the more amorous Librans should have a very good time indeed. If you are settled in your personal attachments you will still want to prove just how important your partner is to you so do something unexpected and flamboyant.

2 WEDNESDAY
Moon Age Day 10   Moon Sign Sagittarius

Romantic possibilities of all kinds are now furthered by the position of Venus in your solar chart. It looks as though you are really being noticed and people find you to be even more attractive than would usually be the case. You also have a strong desire for luxury and for surroundings that are comfortable and opulent.

3 THURSDAY
Moon Age Day 11   Moon Sign Sagittarius

Intimacy is called for by the present planetary line-up and you tend to stick almost exclusively to those people who figure in your life the most. Outsiders won't get into your little world today and you clearly want to be with those you trust. Once again you have the desire to travel, but now in the company of a closed circle.

4 FRIDAY
Moon Age Day 12   Moon Sign Sagittarius

Change and growth is now forecast in your chart, though it tends to come with a fairly spluttering start. Just because ideas don't turn out right immediately doesn't mean you should abandon them out of hand. The adage 'try and try again' is especially appropriate for Libra today, and indeed across the next week or so.

5 SATURDAY
Moon Age Day 13   Moon Sign Capricorn

Domestic and family affairs should prove to be rather rewarding right now, though you also exhibit a fairly restless streak and won't want to stick around the house all day, even though it's Saturday. It doesn't much matter where you go because the important thing is to get a change of scenery. Friends should be happy to go along with you.

6 SUNDAY
Moon Age Day 14   Moon Sign Capricorn

If you are a weekend worker you could be experiencing quite a good time professionally. A spirit of co-operation now exists and this will allow you to find common-sense answers to past problems. There is also a possibility that you will make friends with someone you definitely didn't care for in the past.

7 MONDAY
Moon Age Day 15   Moon Sign Aquarius

You may be spending a lot of time trying to improve things at work, and without much in the way of apparent success. Patience is needed and fortunately that is a commodity you have in buckets. Set your sights on what you want to achieve and move slowly towards it. You will win out in the end.

8 TUESDAY
Moon Age Day 16   Moon Sign Aquarius

Work matters could be put under considerable pressure, though probably not as a result of anything you are doing yourself. Situations beyond your control are likely to arise and these will take some careful thought on your part. Once again you prove yourself equal to almost any task and won't be short of good ideas.

9 WEDNESDAY
Moon Age Day 17   Moon Sign Pisces

A family discussion might help to clear up one or two misunderstandings and could lead to a better way forward, especially with regard to someone who has been rather touchy of late. Bringing things out into the open generally is something you will be inclined to do around this time, and it really helps to clear the air.

10 THURSDAY
Moon Age Day 18   Moon Sign Pisces

There are potential new social interests on the way. Maybe you are going to take up some new form of pastime or hobby or it could be that you are simply mixing with a different group of people. Don't forget that this is August and therefore high summer. Get yourself out of the house. A day trip might prove to be entertaining.

11 FRIDAY
Moon Age Day 19   Moon Sign Pisces

You tend to be very gregarious now and the present astrological line-up brings out the actor in you. Even if you are not performing on a real stage it seems that life serves the same purpose for you. This is one of the best days of the month for both expressing yourself and for truly understanding what others are about.

12 SATURDAY
Moon Age Day 20   Moon Sign Aries

Personal plans now receive setbacks as the Moon enters the zodiac sign of Aries and brings you to the lunar low of the month. There are still some very positive planetary positions around and you are quite well supported in a financial sense. However you might feel slightly down in the dumps for a few hours.

13 SUNDAY
☿   *Moon Age Day 21   Moon Sign Aries*

Guard against sloppy and impractical thinking today and make sure that whatever you do is undertaken properly. If you are at work today, you will need to check your own work and that of others because there is a distinct chance that mistakes can be made. Away from the professional scene your home life should be proving more comfortable.

14 MONDAY
☿   *Moon Age Day 22   Moon Sign Taurus*

This would be a good time to evaluate existing romantic attachments and to ask yourself whether they are working out in quite the way you would wish. Now is certainly the moment to speak your mind, even if this means slightly upsetting someone else. Don't let any sort of difficult situation perpetuate.

15 TUESDAY ☿ *Moon Age Day 23 Moon Sign Taurus*

You now have increased physical energy and tremendous initiative. It's time for Libra to take command, even if one or two people seem less than happy about it. Fortunately you are also very diplomatic at present so you should be able to get yourself adopted as the natural leader, and without any real argument.

16 WEDNESDAY ☿ *Moon Age Day 24 Moon Sign Gemini*

You ought to be able to latch on to better financial trends that come along any time now. This is not an area of life that you will be thinking about exclusively but it does need attention. Friends may prove to be demanding but what they give back is worth any amount of effort on your part today, so don't begrudge the time.

17 THURSDAY ☿ *Moon Age Day 25 Moon Sign Gemini*

Specific astrological trends are still working well on your behalf and they offer you the chance to make progress in areas of life that could have been ignored of late. Comfort and security, never far from the Libran mind, also make an appearance, particularly later in the day. Look out for more solid financial possibilities.

18 FRIDAY ☿ *Moon Age Day 26 Moon Sign Cancer*

Seek the help of those you know can be of assistance today, especially people who are experts in their own particular field. You are confident, though you do recognise that we can't all be good at everything. Practical jobs around the home are one area in which you might elicit some much-needed support.

19 SATURDAY ☿ *Moon Age Day 27 Moon Sign Cancer*

Along comes a day when you will largely be doing your own thing and being just what you wish to be. It's important to be comfortable, even if that means making one or two adjustments early in the day. You won't mind catching up with a few routines, just as long as you can do so at your own pace.

20 SUNDAY ☿ *Moon Age Day 28 Moon Sign Leo*

Your considerable charm now assists you to get ahead anywhere. In reality you are no different today from usual, except for the fact that you are laying on the compliments with a trowel and should be making the best of impressions on practically everyone you meet. It shouldn't be difficult to get on side with superiors.

21 MONDAY ☿ *Moon Age Day 29 Moon Sign Leo*

Creative potential is highlighted and this is a time when you will want to make things look good. Although this trend probably applies most to your domestic surroundings it also has a bearing on your personal appearance. Don't be surprised if you become the centre of attention later in the day, and for all the right reasons.

22 TUESDAY ☿ *Moon Age Day 0 Moon Sign Virgo*

Try to avoid all mood swings, particularly when you are dealing with family members or friends who simply don't seem to be doing what you would wish. Concentrate instead on new ways of getting ahead and on your work, which is very important at present. Socially speaking you should ring the changes as often as possible.

23 WEDNESDAY ☿ *Moon Age Day 1 Moon Sign Virgo*

Now you find much of interest going on in the outside world. With your attention being drawn away from the domestic core of your life a more gregarious sort of Libran begins to show. This part of the week is filled with opportunity and you should make yourself available to much of what is on offer.

24 THURSDAY ☿ *Moon Age Day 2 Moon Sign Virgo*

Friends could prove to be helpful in some fairly unexpected ways. Don't turn down their offers of support, even when you slightly doubt their sincerity. Although you are generally a good judge of character it is possible for you to be wrong sometimes. By the evening you should be in the market for fun.

25 FRIDAY ☿ *Moon Age Day 3 Moon Sign Libra*

This is a great day for making tracks with special plans and for showing those around you just how capable you are. Don't let recent efforts slip, and do what you can to enjoy the social and sporting trends today. Money matters should also be looking better, perhaps with offers you didn't expect coming along.

26 SATURDAY ☿ *Moon Age Day 4 Moon Sign Libra*

This is a favourable time for group activities or just plain co-operation. Try not to make pointless mistakes. Once again this could come about if you are trying to do too many things at the same time. There is a better fluidity in your actions when it comes to social encounters and even romance. The lunar high should be helpful.

27 SUNDAY ☿ *Moon Age Day 5 Moon Sign Scorpio*

Certain ambitious projects tend to wind down at this time, though others almost immediately replace them. Think about priorities in life and stick to these whenever you can. If you are presently on some sort of health kick you should now find yourself reaping the rewards of your efforts.

28 MONDAY ☿ *Moon Age Day 6 Moon Sign Scorpio*

A little good fortune is now on the cards, together with a really flexible attitude that is almost certain to see you getting on well in life generally. Don't be in the least surprised if you are being singled out for specific positive treatment. All that is happening is that grateful friends and colleagues are paying you back.

29 TUESDAY ☿ *Moon Age Day 7 Moon Sign Sagittarius*

Exciting events can be happening in and around your home – the only problem being that you may not be there to register them. There is now a greater desire than ever to be looking for fresh fields and pastures new. Whatever you decide to do, take someone along with you to share the fun and to help pay for it.

30 WEDNESDAY ☿ *Moon Age Day 8   Moon Sign Sagittarius*

Romance and social matters keep you well at the forefront of activities today. It might be the middle of the week but you might find yourself longing for the weekend already. If you are feeling out of sorts later in the day, simply rely on the support that proves to be a natural part of your present, elevated, popularity.

31 THURSDAY ☿ *Moon Age Day 9   Moon Sign Sagittarius*

There are opportunities to get ahead in practical matters today but whether or not you take them remains to be seen. One reason you might not is that you are busy with your social life and also concerned to put extra effort into relationships. It is clear that you cannot achieve every objective and will have to pace yourself, at least for today.

September
⟨♎⟩

2017

1 FRIDAY
☿ *Moon Age Day 10   Moon Sign Capricorn*

Where career matters are at stake you will be quite happy to put in that extra bit of effort that can make all the difference. There should be great things happening in your life generally and you are able to make a good impression on people who have influence. In short, you can accomplish almost anything you set out to do.

2 SATURDAY
☿ *Moon Age Day 11   Moon Sign Capricorn*

You need to get on with your work today and won't be happy around people who waste time or who create problems rather than solutions. In almost all aspects of life you show a positive and inspirational face and will be gaining friends wherever you go. Socially speaking you should also be on top at this time.

3 SUNDAY
☿ *Moon Age Day 12   Moon Sign Aquarius*

It seems that you prove yourself to be an excellent organiser and that people will naturally turn to you to get things in their own lives sorted out. You often work long and hard on behalf of others and this is true at present. Perhaps most important today is your fund of good ideas, some of which need to put into action very soon.

4 MONDAY
☿ *Moon Age Day 13   Moon Sign Aquarius*

It will seem to others at the start of this new week that you have a resolution for every problem. Things won't look quite that simple from your point of view but as long as people have faith in your judgement, life is somewhat easier. Don't turn down a romantic offer without thinking about it carefully.

128

5 TUESDAY   ☿ *Moon Age Day 14   Moon Sign Aquarius*

This is a great period for intellectual growth and for interests that bring you into contact with the outside world. Like-minded people seem to be attracted to you under present trends and that is partly because of the air of confidence and purposefulness that you are giving off. Libra is really on a roll at the moment.

6 WEDNESDAY   ☿   *Moon Age Day 15   Moon Sign Pisces*

You work best now if you are in control of whatever you are doing. It isn't presently difficult for you to hand out instructions to others but it is more of a problem if you have to take the lead from people who don't really seem to know what they are doing. It looks as though a little diplomacy is called for to straighten things out.

7 THURSDAY   ☿   *Moon Age Day 16   Moon Sign Pisces*

Your diplomatic talents can bring advantages at work but are also useful when you are dealing with warring family members or friends who just can't get along with each other. People do listen to you, especially at the moment during a phase when it is so easy for you to pour oil on almost any troubled water.

8 FRIDAY   ☿   *Moon Age Day 17   Moon Sign Aries*

The lunar low brings a quieter phase around now and might make it difficult for you to register any particular progress for the moment. Instead of swimming against the stream, it would be better to take life steadily now. There are plenty of people around who will take the strain instead of you and enjoyment is definitely possible.

9 SATURDAY   ☿   *Moon Age Day 18   Moon Sign Aries*

Don't expect to get much done today. The lunar low is inclined to get in the way and prevents you from moving forward in quite the way you might wish. If you get nervy about something you know you are going to have to say, have a little rehearsal. Even in situations where you are shaking, you can still come through.

10 SUNDAY ☿ *Moon Age Day 19 Moon Sign Taurus*

With an ability to adapt yourself to various roles when necessary, you are now extremely versatile and only too willing to fill in for people if they are out of sorts or indisposed. This skill stands you in good stead because it means you are being watched – probably by people who have great influence.

11 MONDAY ☿ *Moon Age Day 20 Moon Sign Taurus*

You are perhaps slightly impatient at the beginning of this week but this isn't necessarily a bad thing. You will put everything you have into your work and won't be diverted from a course of action you know to be right. Someone in your vicinity has news that means very little to them but a great deal to you.

12 TUESDAY ☿ *Moon Age Day 21 Moon Sign Gemini*

It might not be easy for you to put your finger on sources of tension that are developing at home but it is worth that extra bit of effort necessary to find out what it really going on. Bringing others round to your point of view isn't hard and you certainly have what it takes to make your partner or sweetheart very happy indeed.

13 WEDNESDAY *Moon Age Day 22 Moon Sign Gemini*

This is likely to be a fairly constructive period in a practical sense and a time during which you can turn your hand to almost anything. Libra is now so adaptable that you find yourself being actively sought out by many people. Work hard to keep track of the situation and be more selective than usual, if necessary.

14 THURSDAY *Moon Age Day 23 Moon Sign Cancer*

You show your dynamism and enthusiasm, no matter what you decide to do. It is also fair to suggest that you presently do well in situations that might normally cause you some problems. There is a slight tendency at the moment for you to look back to the past but even this is for a reason – it's so that you don't make the same mistakes again.

15 FRIDAY   *Moon Age Day 24   Moon Sign Cancer*

You function best on this particular Friday when you can find your own space and when you are left to get on with jobs in your own way. What won't work very well are those occasions when you are under the direct gaze of someone else all the time or when people are constantly checking your work.

16 SATURDAY   *Moon Age Day 25   Moon Sign Cancer*

A strong creative impulse this weekend can lead you to new interests and it will certainly make you want to do something to beautify your surroundings. You should be sparing time for family members, particularly ones who have been going through a difficult time of late, and also keeping up with a hectic social life.

17 SUNDAY   *Moon Age Day 26   Moon Sign Leo*

It is probably not advisable to believe everything you hear today because there are likely to be a few people around who have some sort of interest in distorting the truth. You might have to let go of something that has been important to you in the distant past but which now has more or less run its course.

18 MONDAY   *Moon Age Day 27   Moon Sign Leo*

Your sunny disposition is on show, as is a more than usually robust constitution and a desire to push the bounds of the credible. As a result a more adventurous Libran is on display and you might decide to try something you have shied away from in the past. Stay away from anything that is definitely dangerous but you can push yourself a little.

19 TUESDAY   *Moon Age Day 28   Moon Sign Virgo*

You simply must have luxurious surroundings if at all possible, a fact that shows itself time and again whilst Venus retains its present position in your solar chart. As a result you are likely to be doing everything you can to keep things tidy and to improve your general décor at home.

20 WEDNESDAY *Moon Age Day 0   Moon Sign Virgo*

Your optimism and cheerfulness under present trends ought to win you many admirers and will also help you to succeed because others are so willing to pitch in on your behalf. You should be feeling fairly good about yourself in a general sense and will want to push the bounds of the credible, especially when work is over.

21 THURSDAY *Moon Age Day 1   Moon Sign Libra*

As far as opportunities are concerned you are entering one of the very best phases for some time. The lunar high is supportive and offers you incentives you wouldn't have expected. What's more you know how to shine in almost any situation and should be more than ready to take the world by storm, particularly this evening.

22 FRIDAY *Moon Age Day 2   Moon Sign Libra*

This is a dynamic and inspirational period, though it is not without an element of risk. Despite the fact that you feel invincible you are probably more vulnerable than you think. Fortunately Libra retains its common sense, even when the planetary influences are so powerful. Excitement can now be your middle name.

23 SATURDAY *Moon Age Day 3   Moon Sign Scorpio*

The weekend will find you anxious to pick up any sort of information, whether it turns out to be useful or not. Indulging in gossip will be something you do without thinking and you will be more attracted than usual to the superficial elements of life. That's fine because you can't be thinking deeply all the time.

24 SUNDAY *Moon Age Day 4   Moon Sign Scorpio*

Today you know how to keep a conversation going because your sense of humour is so well honed. Don't forget that this is the weekend and avoid working all the time, even if your work is enjoyable. You need a few hours to enjoy yourself and you should also spend time with your partner or family members.

25 MONDAY   *Moon Age Day 5   Moon Sign Scorpio*

It looks as though you are now rather eager to be the centre of attention and you can expect a favourable response under the present planetary line-up. Getting on with people is never difficult for you and especially not at this time. You are able to conform to the expectations of your partner and family.

26 TUESDAY   *Moon Age Day 6   Moon Sign Sagittarius*

The place you learn things most quickly at this time will be at work. Not only can you acquire new skills, you are also keeping your ears open, which itself can be very useful. Any temporary negative trends are now receding into the background, which allows you to be as happy and cheerful as seems to have been the case for most of this month.

27 WEDNESDAY   *Moon Age Day 7   Moon Sign Sagittarius*

Travel arrangements may have to be changed, in some cases at the last moment. Don't assume this will necessarily be a bad thing because something quite surprising and delightful might arise as a result. What you need today is flexibility and a willingness to follow circumstances, rather than trying to predict everything yourself.

28 THURSDAY   *Moon Age Day 8   Moon Sign Capricorn*

You certainly have the ability to command attention today and should be turning heads wherever you go. With some positive planetary positions around, and others developing, you are more progressive and should feel generally better in yourself. This is not lost on those around you who recognise your cheerful ways.

29 FRIDAY   *Moon Age Day 9   Moon Sign Capricorn*

A significant focus on domestic issues and home life in general should make for a reasonably comfortable sort of day. Your ideas are not quite so grandiose as they have been across the last two or three weeks, but you are gentle and caring. A couple of calculated gambles could pay off today.

30 SATURDAY   *Moon Age Day 10   Moon Sign Capricorn*

There are some potentially interesting encounters around during the weekend, though not of course if you insist on staying behind closed doors. Now you need to spread your wings and there are people around you who will be only too willing to take a trip somewhere special with you. Make a real fuss of your partner this weekend.

October 2017

1 SUNDAY
Moon Age Day 11   Moon Sign Aquarius

This could be a very confusing and tense time as far as your personal life is concerned but only if you fail to look at things in an objective and honest manner. You could easily be worrying about something without any evidence or justification and that means dissipating otherwise useful energy to no real purpose.

2 MONDAY
Moon Age Day 12   Moon Sign Aquarius

An exciting and adventurous couple of days lie before you. There are some really good planetary influences, all of which are urging you onwards towards new incentives and activities. With no time to hang around you will be showing the world who is boss right now and few would stand in your way.

3 TUESDAY
Moon Age Day 13   Moon Sign Pisces

Progress in your career depends on your ability to think down completely new channels. Libra is certainly on the ball at the moment but there is a tendency for you to sometimes get stuck in your way of thinking. The more revolutionary you are at present, the greater is the chance that the world will take notice.

4 WEDNESDAY
Moon Age Day 14   Moon Sign Pisces

Your critical faculties are excellent and it would take someone very clever indeed to fool you at the moment. That makes this an ideal time for looking at and signing documents of any sort and for embarking on a new project that is going to demand a great deal of your time and attention in the weeks ahead.

135

5 THURSDAY
Moon Age Day 15   Moon Sign Aries

Basically the lunar low brings a slight downer and a time during which you might as well take a well-earned break. Not everything you do is going wrong but it will be hard to make any significant headway and it might be best not to push yourself. Colleagues will fill the breach for you and friends are supportive too.

6 FRIDAY
Moon Age Day 16   Moon Sign Aries

Today could be slightly characterised by confusion - that is unless you take one job at a time and think things through carefully before you commit yourself to anything at all. Fortunately there is likely to be a great deal of good humour about too, together with the company of people who have the ability to make you laugh out loud.

7 SATURDAY
Moon Age Day 17   Moon Sign Taurus

It is towards your friends that you tend to look for a good time this weekend. Formal situations are not significant and you may prefer to make up your mind as you go along when it comes to enjoyment. The more spontaneous you are, the greater is the chance that you encounter one of those very special times that cannot be planned.

8 SUNDAY
Moon Age Day 18   Moon Sign Taurus

Personal relationships and partnerships of all sorts can now bring much more than you bargained for, though generally in a very positive sense. Your powers of attraction are clearly very strong at the moment so don't be afraid to use them to your own advantage. Just don't lead someone up the garden path romantically.

9 MONDAY
Moon Age Day 19   Moon Sign Taurus

Romantic and social activities can represent a welcome diversion, especially since you are not in the mood to commit yourself exclusively to work. This would be an excellent time to bury the hatchet as far as a long-standing disagreement or row is concerned and you will also be playing the honest broker for others.

10 TUESDAY
Moon Age Day 20   Moon Sign Gemini

You have a very fertile mind at the best of times but now it is truly active. Intuition is strong and you can afford to back your hunches to a much greater extent than has been the case in the very recent past. Life is now much more about feelings than evidence, though this might be hard for some Librans to appreciate.

11 WEDNESDAY
Moon Age Day 21   Moon Sign Gemini

At this time the focus is clearly on your personal life and though you remain generally busy in a practical sense, much of your time is likely to be spent in the company of your partner, sorting things out and proving the depth of your affection. All this effort is certainly not wasted and there is great love coming back in your direction.

12 THURSDAY
Moon Age Day 22   Moon Sign Cancer

Changes to your financial situation can give you more ease and comfort in your surroundings, though this is likely to be a gradual process that takes place over the next few weeks. For now you are likely to be happy. Libra is definitely in the mood for a spot of shopping or a trip to visit relatives or friends.

13 FRIDAY
Moon Age Day 23   Moon Sign Cancer

You function well when it comes to looking after your own interests, especially in a financial sense. However it is quite important at the moment that you do not allow a sudden fondness for detail to get in your way at a time when a broad overview is far more useful. Colleagues should be very helpful around now.

14 SATURDAY
Moon Age Day 24   Moon Sign Leo

People notice you this weekend, mainly because of the positive way you express yourself. It is easy to make others feel important and to encourage them to work hard on your behalf. Routines are not appealing and you long to ring the changes whenever it proves to be possible. A late holiday might be in order.

15 SUNDAY   *Moon Age Day 25   Moon Sign Leo*

Make the most of a good period for romance and do what you can to sweep someone completely off their feet. Social relationships should also be very good and will offer you the chance of new friendships, one or two of which might endure for a very long time. This is not to suggest that you ignore old friends, all of whom remain important.

16 MONDAY   *Moon Age Day 26   Moon Sign Virgo*

Handling a heavy workload won't bother you at all as the week gets started though this situation can change significantly as the days go on so make the most of this positive beginning. Clear the decks for action that comes at the far end of the week but don't plan anything too strenuous if family commitments are looming.

17 TUESDAY   *Moon Age Day 27   Moon Sign Virgo*

You definitely enjoy being busy today and can make the best out of almost any sort of circumstance. Watch out for the odd minor mishap, probably brought about as a result of carelessness exhibited by someone else. Your present quick thinking makes you good to have around in any tight corner.

18 WEDNESDAY   *Moon Age Day 28   Moon Sign Libra*

You work best now when at the centre of lots of activity. The hotter the situation the better you will enjoy it and the cut and thrust of life is what keeps you really busy whilst the lunar high is around. Most important of all at present is your ability to get through or around problems that once seemed impossible to solve.

19 THURSDAY   *Moon Age Day 29   Moon Sign Libra*

This is the time to push boundaries and to try things out before you decide you are not equal to the task. You can achieve victories now that would have seemed absolutely impossible just a short while ago and won't be at all fazed by any sort of opposition. Libra is unusually fearless at the moment.

20 FRIDAY
Moon Age Day 0   Moon Sign Libra

The practical world is still doing you the odd favour, allowing you to make gains, particularly in a financial sense. Rules and regulations are not too difficult to follow now and you find yourself well able to conform when it is necessary. Help a friend with a problem and also be supportive of family members.

21 SATURDAY
Moon Age Day 1   Moon Sign Scorpio

It seems that love is mainly where your interests are centred on this October Saturday. You relish the company of someone who cares about you deeply and will do almost anything in return. In more casual attachments, you may be rather confused by the attitude of people who seem self-destructive and who won't take advice.

22 SUNDAY
Moon Age Day 2   Moon Sign Scorpio

You can probably expect a great deal of positive attention coming your way around this time. This will happen in both a personal and in a more general sense. Popularity is everything to you now and you won't hold back in terms of the love you offer in return. Almost anyone can feel your warmth during this most fascinating period.

23 MONDAY
Moon Age Day 3   Moon Sign Sagittarius

It won't be difficult for you to work with people in authority at the moment. You are compliant and more than willing to co-operate, just as long as you consider that the suggestions being made are sensible. There could be some irritations about but these are most likely caused by determination on your part that cannot be utilised yet.

24 TUESDAY
Moon Age Day 4   Moon Sign Sagittarius

This is likely to be a very busy day, even if you are not committed to working. There are gains to be made in your financial dealings and you will probably also be more in tune with family members who have caused you one or two problems recently. Don't wait to be asked in any situation that appeals to you but go for it.

25 WEDNESDAY *Moon Age Day 5   Moon Sign Sagittarius*

You get even more from being on the go today. The Moon is in a good position for you and should prove to be especially helpful when it comes to expressing your emotions. This would be an excellent time for a heart-to-heart with your partner and you are in a good position to think up the sort of compliments that make a difference.

26 THURSDAY *Moon Age Day 6   Moon Sign Capricorn*

As far as your career is concerned you are now likely to go it alone to a greater extent than would normally be the case. This is either because you can't find the advice you need or else because colleagues are not proving quite as reliable as you would wish. Even Libra can be very single-minded and this is certainly the case around now.

27 FRIDAY *Moon Age Day 7   Moon Sign Capricorn*

This is a day when you will be quite happy to be noticed – in fact you are setting your stall out specifically to make sure that you are. You will want to look your best and to attract the sort of people you find alluring and fascinating. Libra is actually quite sexy under present trends and of your attraction to others there will be no doubt.

28 SATURDAY *Moon Age Day 8   Moon Sign Aquarius*

Progress in your daily life is no more than steady today but that doesn't mean you fail to make any headway at all. Prior planning is important, together with getting little details sorted out that will make your path easier in a day or two. However, you will have to be patient as far as practical movement is concerned.

29 SUNDAY *Moon Age Day 9   Moon Sign Aquarius*

Today should be quite light-hearted and demands a very gentle touch. Any tendency to get too serious about anything won't meet with a good response from others, so show just how humorous and jolly you are capable of being. This is especially necessary in personal attachments and with regard to romance.

30 MONDAY

Moon Age Day 10   Moon Sign Pisces

This will be one of the best days of the week for busy preparations and for making sure that everything you need is in place for your plans to mature later. If you are working on several different fronts at the same time you could find yourself running out of steam if you also go for a very hectic social time this evening.

31 TUESDAY

Moon Age Day 11   Moon Sign Pisces

You may have your work cut out today in solving problems that are caused, in the main, by colleagues or even friends. Most situations will be quite easy to deal with and you tend to approach life with a very good attitude. If anyone is the joker in the pack around this time it is almost certain to be you.

♎ November 2017

1 WEDNESDAY
Moon Age Day 12   Moon Sign Pisces

It's already the first day of November and you will probably be left wondering where much of the year has actually gone. If you look back though, you should see just how far you have come in many respects and you are still planning events and gatherings that will fall within this year. Try to remain as optimistic as possible today.

2 THURSDAY
Moon Age Day 13   Moon Sign Aries

The arrival of the lunar low is inclined to put the brakes on as far as some of your more practical efforts are concerned and you could quite easily discover that a slower and steadier approach is called for. People in the know are in a good position to offer you some sound advice and right now you have sufficient time to listen to them.

3 FRIDAY
Moon Age Day 14   Moon Sign Aries

Life can seem fairly demanding, whilst at the same time failing to offer you quite the same incentives you have come to expect of late. Everything you get seems to come hard but at least you are applying yourself and won't be easily beaten. In some situations it might be that you are trying just a little too hard.

4 SATURDAY
Moon Age Day 15   Moon Sign Taurus

There is a slightly testing phase on the way for your partnerships, whether these are of a personal or a professional sort. It looks as though you are inclined to go solo for the moment and that might be part of what is causing the potential problems. This is out of character because you are usually so good at sharing.

5 SUNDAY
Moon Age Day 16   Moon Sign Taurus

You will benefit greatly today from getting together with others and discussing almost anything under the sun. Some of the best answers you find at the moment can come as a result of these discussions and since you are in a very 'think tank' mentality, the more people you draw into your circle, the better the results should be.

6 MONDAY
Moon Age Day 17   Moon Sign Gemini

Partnerships are likely to take up a great deal of your time as you work hard to bring someone round to a point of view that seems quite self-evident to you. No matter how hard you try, you may have difficulty persuading people to follow your lead and if this is the case you will have to work especially hard to find a compromise.

7 TUESDAY
Moon Age Day 18   Moon Sign Gemini

The big lesson to learn today is that you cannot and should not exert a possessive influence on those close to you. It is not the right way forward to try to make them change to suit your needs and in any case you will be more likely to have a positive influence on them if you allow them to decide for themselves.

8 WEDNESDAY
Moon Age Day 19   Moon Sign Cancer

A period of some mental pressure comes along, but probably only because you have so many potential choices to make. Try not to dwell too much on specific issues and allow your intuition to be at least part of your guide. This is because your usual common sense might not be enough to get you the answers you need.

9 THURSDAY
Moon Age Day 20   Moon Sign Cancer

Good communications with relatives and with your partner will be needed today if you are to solve a slight problem or series of problems that will become obvious at home. There is a great deal to be said at the moment for sticking with a few routines and also for allowing others to take some of the strain.

10 FRIDAY
Moon Age Day 21   Moon Sign Leo

This might not be the most romantic period of the month but it does offer certain benefits that have a bearing on personal attachments. You are a good talker and also a great listener around this time. Because you are so attentive people who tend to have kept things somewhat hidden for a while should now open up.

11 SATURDAY
Moon Age Day 22   Moon Sign Leo

Paradoxically for those of you who do not work at the weekend, today offers some of the very best professional prospects of the week. You are quite decisive now and won't leave anything to chance. Domestic prospects are very slightly less rosy, perhaps because those around you are tetchy or inclined to be over-critical about something.

12 SUNDAY
Moon Age Day 23   Moon Sign Virgo

This is a time during which you can capitalise on your ability to do something novel or different. Getting out to places of culture and learning something on the way could prove to be very important to Libra under present trends. What's more, you are inspiring others with your refreshing attitudes and your deep knowledge.

13 MONDAY
Moon Age Day 24   Moon Sign Virgo

Expect a fairly unsettled period early in the week. People you meet in a professional or social sense don't seem to be making much sense and you will constantly have to make allowances for them. Nothing feels reliable to you and the only time things go the way you would expect is when you attend to them yourself.

14 TUESDAY
Moon Age Day 25   Moon Sign Libra

Today have an awareness of your individuality and you won't be at all inclined to stay in the background. Wherever there is action, that is where you will choose to be because Libra is now about as dynamic and driven as it is possible for the zodiac sign to be. It should be relatively easy to get your own way.

15 WEDNESDAY   *Moon Age Day 26   Moon Sign Libra*

You now have quite an unusual response to what life offers you, with the result that you are living your life in a fairly unique way. The attraction you have for others isn't at all in doubt and you can turn heads wherever you go. This period isn't all about work because from a social point of view you can sizzle.

16 THURSDAY   *Moon Age Day 27   Moon Sign Libra*

Your personal life is emphasised now and you will probably be concentrating on those issues that are going to make you feel happier and more contented in the weeks and months ahead. Family discussions could be on the cards and there are positive gains to be made from knowing how others feel.

17 FRIDAY   *Moon Age Day 28   Moon Sign Scorpio*

Something about today might make you feel let down. If this is the case you can be sure that the root of this feeling is mental and emotional because there probably will not be anything going wrong in a practical sense. It's up to you to keep pushing forward and to ignore the fact that you may be feeling slightly down.

18 SATURDAY   *Moon Age Day 0   Moon Sign Scorpio*

This will be a time of great insight, when your intuitive nature works overtime. When it comes to assessing others you will now be second to none and you won't easily be fooled, either in a practical or a personal sense. There may be significant room for compromise regarding a disagreement somewhere in the family.

19 SUNDAY   *Moon Age Day 1   Moon Sign Sagittarius*

Those you meet socially will stimulate your own thinking and may bring you to alternative strategies and ingenious ideas that were not in place only a day or two ago. Mentally speaking you will be as bright as a button and it would take someone extremely clever to get one over on you. Your cognitive skills are now excellent.

20 MONDAY   *Moon Age Day 2   Moon Sign Sagittarius*

This is a time of excitement and change – a period when you can't necessarily wait for others to keep up and when you will be very keen to follow the dictates of your own will. Of course there are occasions when you can't ignore the needs of those around you but with your present ingenuity you can somehow incorporate them.

21 TUESDAY   *Moon Age Day 3   Moon Sign Sagittarius*

You like to be noticed and will probably be actively doing things to make sure that you are not overlooked. When it comes to getting what you want in a professional sense, commitment and intent are both extremely important at the moment. You seem to have a knowing knack of being in the right place at the right time.

22 WEDNESDAY   *Moon Age Day 4   Moon Sign Capricorn*

Life is not a rehearsal, as you are about to discover. Instead of waiting around to see what might happen, today is a time to get busy and to make things mature in the way you would wish. There is no end to your own power under present trends but it all depends on your own attitude and your willingness to become involved.

23 THURSDAY   *Moon Age Day 5   Moon Sign Capricorn*

Right at this moment in time you want to be number one. Since you rarely have a selfish bone in your body there is nothing at all wrong with being self-centred once in a while. What's more, you should discover that those who care about you the most will be anxious to let you have your own way. Even some strangers might join in.

24 FRIDAY   *Moon Age Day 6   Moon Sign Aquarius*

You should now be on a winning streak in a professional sense and it looks as though you will be readily acting upon new opportunities that come your way. This part of November could turn out to be quite exciting and to offer possibilities that would have seemed out of the question even a few short months ago.

25 SATURDAY *Moon Age Day 7   Moon Sign Aquarius*

You continue to seek adventure, though now you tend to do so through romance. If you have more than one admirer at the moment you might be busy doing some sort of balancing act! Even Librans who feel themselves to be settled in a romantic sense could find the flame of love burning much brighter.

26 SUNDAY *Moon Age Day 8   Moon Sign Aquarius*

Don't be distracted by the demands made upon you by friends and family members. Although you may have time to think about domestic issues on a Sunday, at the same time there is plenty of potential excitement about too. It might be necessary to split your day but avoid giving yourself entirely to anything tedious or demanding.

27 MONDAY *Moon Age Day 9   Moon Sign Pisces*

Leave behind anything that is inclined to drag you down. This might seem the worst time of the year for a spring clean in the general sense of the expression but as far as your mind goes, this is the best period of all. A new year is not that far away and you don't want to carry too much surplus baggage on into December.

28 TUESDAY *Moon Age Day 10   Moon Sign Pisces*

Powerful emotions are stirred up in your mind and it is towards home and family that most of your thinking is directed. Beware of frayed tempers and don't put yourself in a position where others will accuse you of being bossy. Beware, also, a couple of trends that mean a little temper is in evidence when you are at home.

29 WEDNESDAY *Moon Age Day 11   Moon Sign Aries*

This may not be the luckiest day of the month, especially in any practical sense. You have the lunar low to cope with and this can take the wind out of your sails in a number of different ways. Rely on what others can do for you and take some rest. You will be back up to speed before you know it but rushing today won't help.

30 THURSDAY   *Moon Age Day 12   Moon Sign Aries*

This is another day that more or less demands you take things at a calmer pace and don't get involved in issues that will sap your energy and resolve. You will tire easily at the moment, which is why you need to watch and wait. By tomorrow things should be back to normal, but for the moment simply relax.

♎ December

2017

1 FRIDAY
Moon Age Day 13   Moon Sign Taurus

It looks as though you will have your detective hat on today. Just about everything interests you but what stands out is your present rampant curiosity. When it comes to working out why things happen in the way they do you will leave no stone unturned – and you are likely to have a good time on the way.

2 SATURDAY
Moon Age Day 14   Moon Sign Taurus

For a number of planetary reasons your interests now tend to turn towards mental and philosophical considerations. Some Librans will even by gaining a new spiritual dimension to their lives or else embarking on some sort of health kick that brings intellectual depth as well as stronger muscles. Don't push yourself too hard.

3 SUNDAY
☿   *Moon Age Day 15   Moon Sign Gemini*

A new phase is underway and it is one that may challenge you to renew and revitalise certain aspects of your life that have become dull or unworkable. Of necessity this means leaving something behind and that isn't necessarily easy for Libra. Excess baggage isn't important though and it is getting in your way.

4 MONDAY
☿   *Moon Age Day 16   Moon Sign Gemini*

Self-criticism at the start of this working week can stem from too great an expectation of yourself and your recent efforts. A more modest approach to situations seems to be called for, together with a greater ability to relax into life. The more content you make yourself, the better most aspects of your life will seem to be.

149

5 TUESDAY ☿ *Moon Age Day 17 Moon Sign Cancer*

You may discover today how important it is to plan your next strategy because certain situations will unravel like a ball of wool if you trust to luck. This need not be a problem because Libra is now about as organised as any zodiac sign can be. Unforced errors are not very likely but concentration is still necessary.

6 WEDNESDAY ☿ *Moon Age Day 18 Moon Sign Cancer*

You can get what you want today with the aid of a little persuasion and you won't easily be put off by the slightly negative attitudes of people with whom you have to deal. Avoid getting involved in arguments of any sort but particularly those that you know instinctively are going to lead you nowhere at all.

7 THURSDAY ☿ *Moon Age Day 19 Moon Sign Leo*

The way ahead now looks fairly clear, though you view it from a sort of platform and won't be putting in too much in the way of direct physical effort for the moment. For some days now you should have been ridding yourself of baggage that you don't want to carry forward into the coming year. Expect some new incentives to come along, too.

8 FRIDAY ☿ *Moon Age Day 20 Moon Sign Leo*

It would be a great advantage today to continue your general efforts to get on well – but whilst also learning the value of relaxation. The situation is helped if you tackle one task at a time and don't crowd yourself with tasks that aren't at all necessary. You can also get on better if you learn to delegate.

9 SATURDAY ☿ *Moon Age Day 21 Moon Sign Virgo*

You might now have to rethink a pet project very carefully, especially if it is becoming obvious to you that something isn't working in the way you had hoped. There is no point at all in ploughing on regardless, when a slight alteration to the way you behave can make all the difference.

10 SUNDAY ☿ *Moon Age Day 22   Moon Sign Virgo*

Your love of travel is likely to show itself and you will soon feel dull and disinterested if you don't get some change into almost every aspect of your life. What started out as a little restlessness has now become something much more. Avoid unnecessary routines and opt for as many diversions as you can find.

11 MONDAY ☿ *Moon Age Day 23   Moon Sign Virgo*

You may feel compelled to move forward, probably at work, even if other people seem to be dragging their feet. It seems as if there is no stopping you at the moment and you rise to challenges in a moment. At home you may decide to make alterations to décor or change things round in some way, maybe ahead of Christmas.

12 TUESDAY ☿ *Moon Age Day 24   Moon Sign Libra*

Your sense of timing is impeccable and you will be anxious to make headway in practical matters. You should now be less geared towards negative thoughts and on the contrary your mind can concentrate on very positive issues to do with career and money. There is a stronger element of good luck attending your actions.

13 WEDNESDAY ☿ *Moon Age Day 25   Moon Sign Libra*

Your mind is working overtime and you have sufficient energy at the moment for your body to keep up. Your health seems to be in good shape and if there have been any issues in that direction recently, these could now be resolved. All things considered, this should be the most positive time of the month for you.

14 THURSDAY ☿ *Moon Age Day 26   Moon Sign Scorpio*

Avoid conflicts in your love life by refusing to get involved in pointless discussions or even arguments. It isn't you who is being reactive but rather those around you, but you could so easily be drawn into rows. For most of the time you are as calm and easy-going as anything but you can display a stubborn streak right now.

15 FRIDAY ☿ *Moon Age Day 27   Moon Sign Scorpio*

Today could be especially good for all business matters, since you display a healthy mix of optimism and caution. This is Libra at its best and it stands you in good stead when it comes to making money. Planning projects should be easy and you have such a good understanding with colleagues at present they should follow your lead.

16 SATURDAY ☿ *Moon Age Day 28   Moon Sign Scorpio*

Romance could bring a little tension on this particular Saturday and you will need to make sure you don't take offence over something that isn't really important. There are challenges to be faced if you are at work, though these tend to be quite positive in nature. It's important for the moment not to react too harshly to nothing in particular.

17 SUNDAY ☿ *Moon Age Day 29   Moon Sign Sagittarius*

Your interest in travel, which has been increasing steadily throughout this month, is now getting quite intense. You actively need fresh fields and pastures new, even though those around you might have very different ideas. Short trips will do the trick for a while but what you really want is a long and luxurious holiday. Fat chance!

18 MONDAY ☿ *Moon Age Day 0   Moon Sign Sagittarius*

A little soul searching may be necessary in order for you to come to terms with certain aspects of your life as they appear now. In your anxiety to make almost everything different there is a very real chance you might throw out the baby with the bathwater. You might have to put on the brakes a little after making conscious decisions.

19 TUESDAY ☿ *Moon Age Day 1   Moon Sign Capricorn*

A sense of co-operation that probably did not exist a few days ago now makes itself felt. You have an upbeat emotional outlook and will be far less likely to get involved in disputes that lead to arguments. The Moon is in a useful position for you at the moment and that turns out to be especially good when dealing with your family.

20 WEDNESDAY ☿ *Moon Age Day 2   Moon Sign Capricorn*

A personal issue may show the extent to which you have your work cut out. This can be quite a reactive sort of day but you should still make progress and enjoy yourself if you approach matters in the right way. Stop and think before you make momentous decisions and do your best to avoid cluttering up your life with pointless items.

21 THURSDAY ☿ *Moon Age Day 3   Moon Sign Capricorn*

You have a strong drive to make a good impression all round. If you are meeting new people, which is quite likely, you will want to put in the extra effort to make the most of what could turn out to be deep friendships. Don't get too involved in the personal problems of a friend. Give advice but stay away from intrigue.

22 FRIDAY ☿ *Moon Age Day 4   Moon Sign Aquarius*

There is some strong support to be had today, particularly at work. It looks as though you will be busy but that isn't too surprising with Christmas only a few days away. Take some time out to remember all those people for whom you haven't bought presents and do something about it today.

23 SATURDAY *Moon Age Day 5   Moon Sign Aquarius*

You can make some progress at work, that is if you happen to work at the weekend, but otherwise this should be a fairly steady sort of day. The chances are that you will be preparing yourself for the upcoming festivities and you can enjoy a fairly settled family time if you put your mind to it. There is still some restlessness about.

24 SUNDAY *Moon Age Day 6   Moon Sign Pisces*

Today brings a steady start but with a rapid improvement as the day moves on. Christmas Eve should find you anxious to move about freely, less held back by details and more inclined to get out there and have a good time. Last minute details can be sorted out and you have a great ability to create fun at the drop of a hat.

25 MONDAY
Moon Age Day 7   Moon Sign Pisces

Travel is positively highlighted for Christmas Day, so maybe at least part of the day will be spent somewhere other than in your own home. Whether this proves to be the case or not you are likely to be very cheerful and quite imaginative. Your present attitude is just right for having fun yourself and promoting it for others.

26 TUESDAY
Moon Age Day 8   Moon Sign Pisces

When you are involved in discussions today you could find that the people around you are proving to be more argumentative than you may have expected. Keep your patience and to explain yourself as fully as you can. If things still don't go the way you want you must either compromise or else do your own thing.

27 WEDNESDAY
Moon Age Day 9   Moon Sign Aries

There is every reason to feel left behind today as you enter the lunar low for December. It might be slightly trying but at least you will get this less-than-favourable phase out of the way before New Year arrives. Stand and stare for a while, whilst you let other people do some jobs for you. This isn't selfish – it's sensible.

28 THURSDAY
Moon Age Day 10   Moon Sign Aries

Expect anything but smooth progress, even though the things that go wrong are not really important. Frustrations may be evident and you should take special care if you have to start anything new at this time. Seek expert advice from people who know what they are talking about and avoid all cowboys!

29 FRIDAY
Moon Age Day 11   Moon Sign Taurus

Be open to new input today and allow yourself the right to change your mind if you know instinctively it is necessary to do so. This might involve you in some fairly deep discussions in order to explain yourself but you have a silver tongue at the moment and won't have any trouble getting others to agree with you.

30 SATURDAY   *Moon Age Day 12   Moon Sign Taurus*

Romantic issues may throw up the odd challenge so pay attention in order to make certain you are saying and doing the right things. It might seem as if there are tests around now, custom-made to make sure that you are thinking and acting in the right way. Some new hobby or pastime could be on the cards.

31 SUNDAY   *Moon Age Day 13   Moon Sign Gemini*

You are certainly not a shrinking violet as the year draws towards its close. You intend to be fully in the social and personal spotlight and that is where you will undoubtedly feel most comfortable at the moment. Compliments come from many different directions – though you might be too busy to notice them.